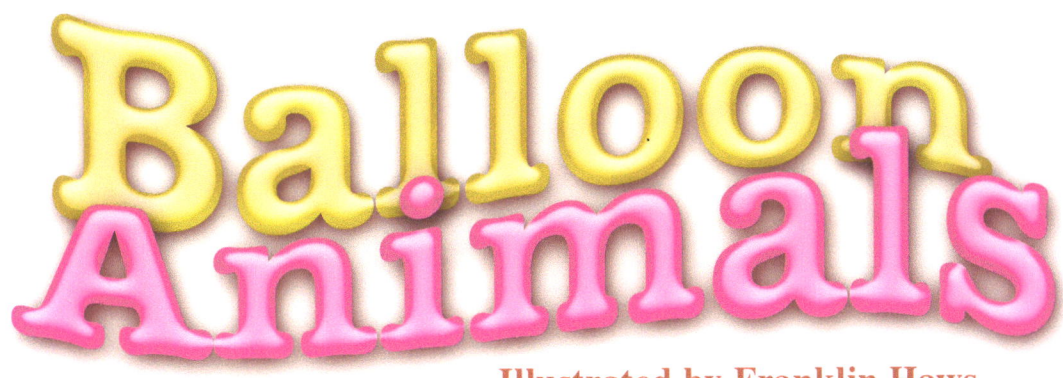

Balloon Animals

Illustrated by Franklin Haws

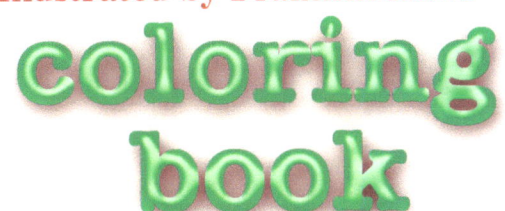

coloring book

**Dedicated to all the
budding artists
young and old.**

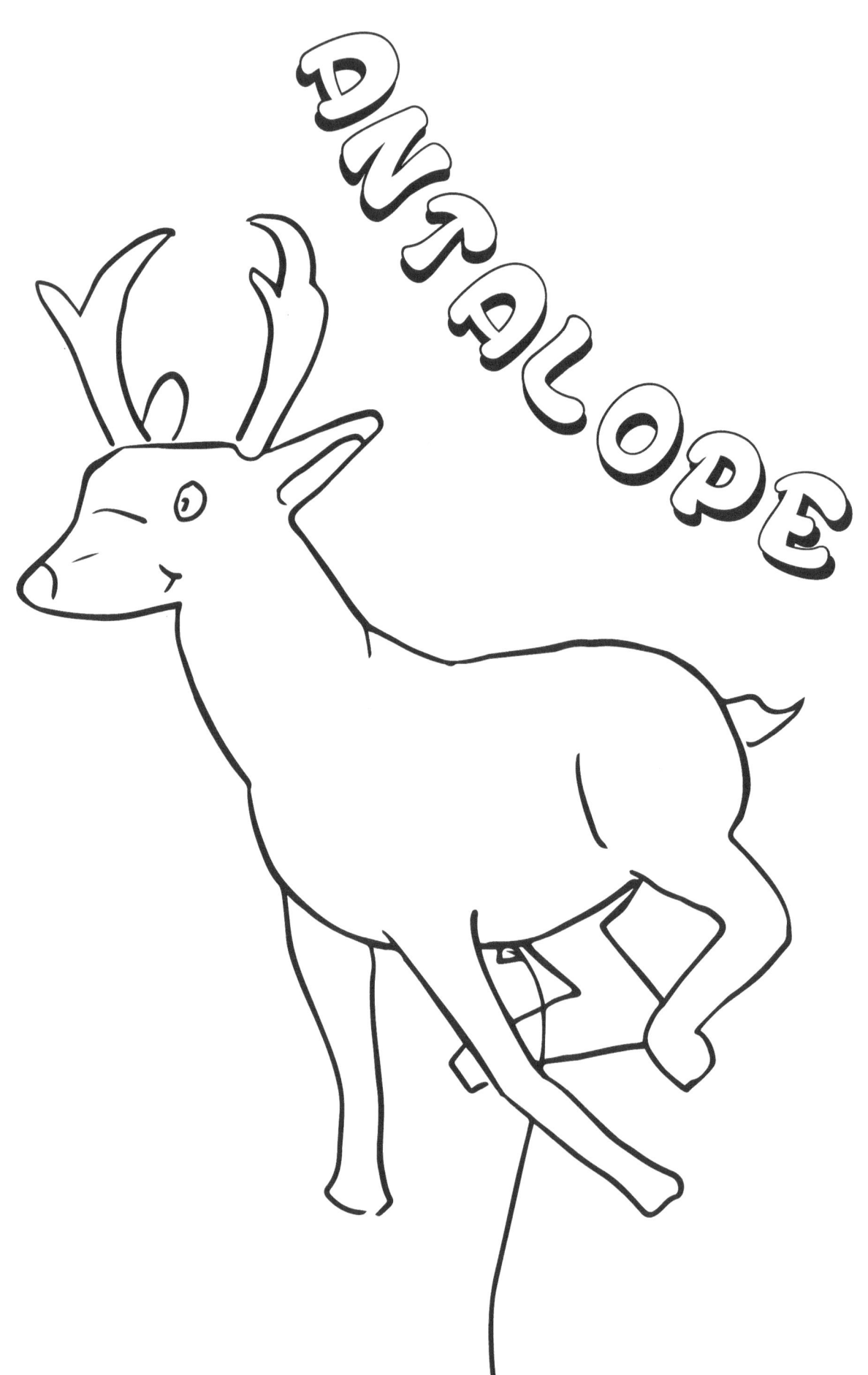

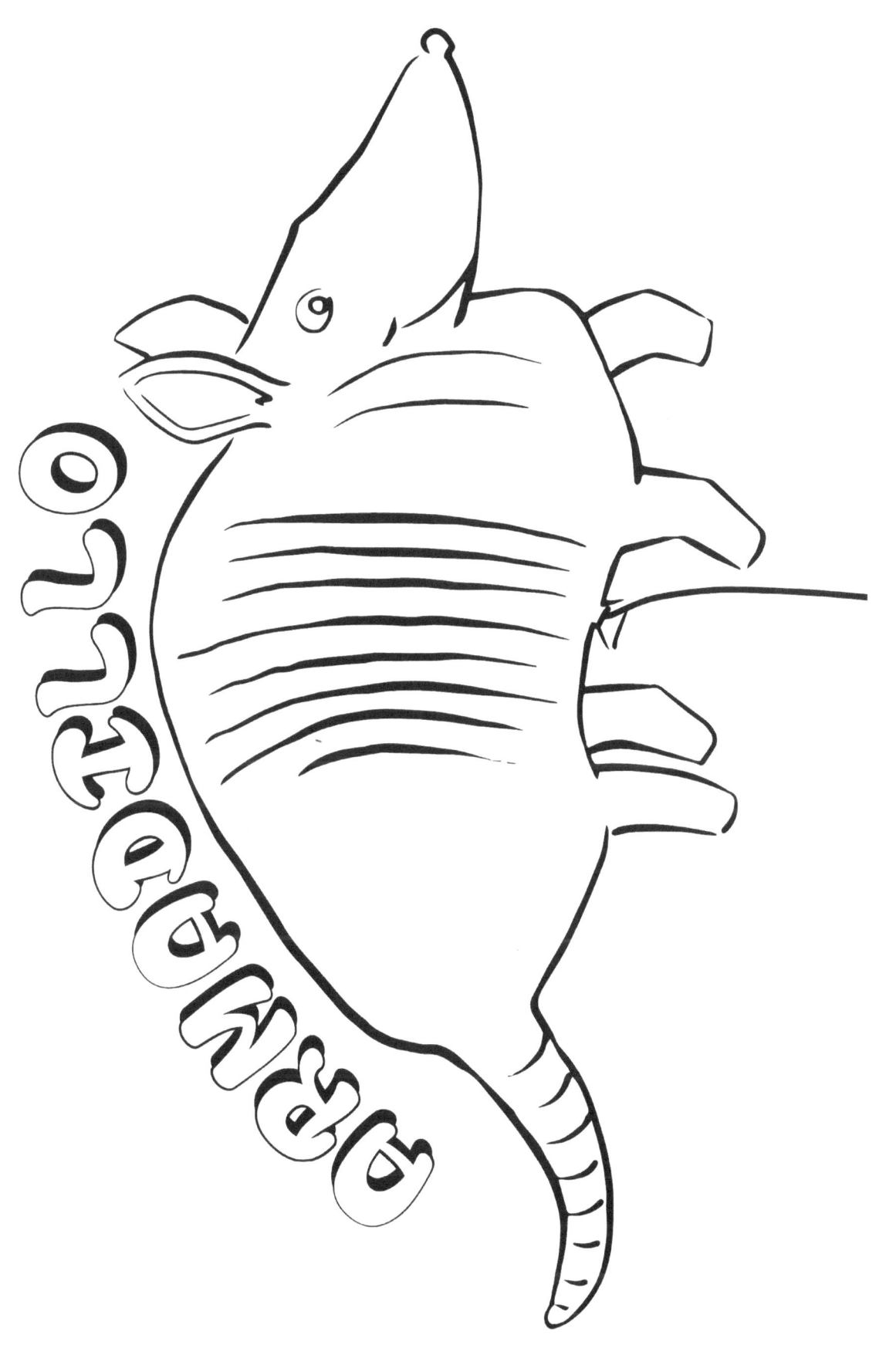

ARMADILLO

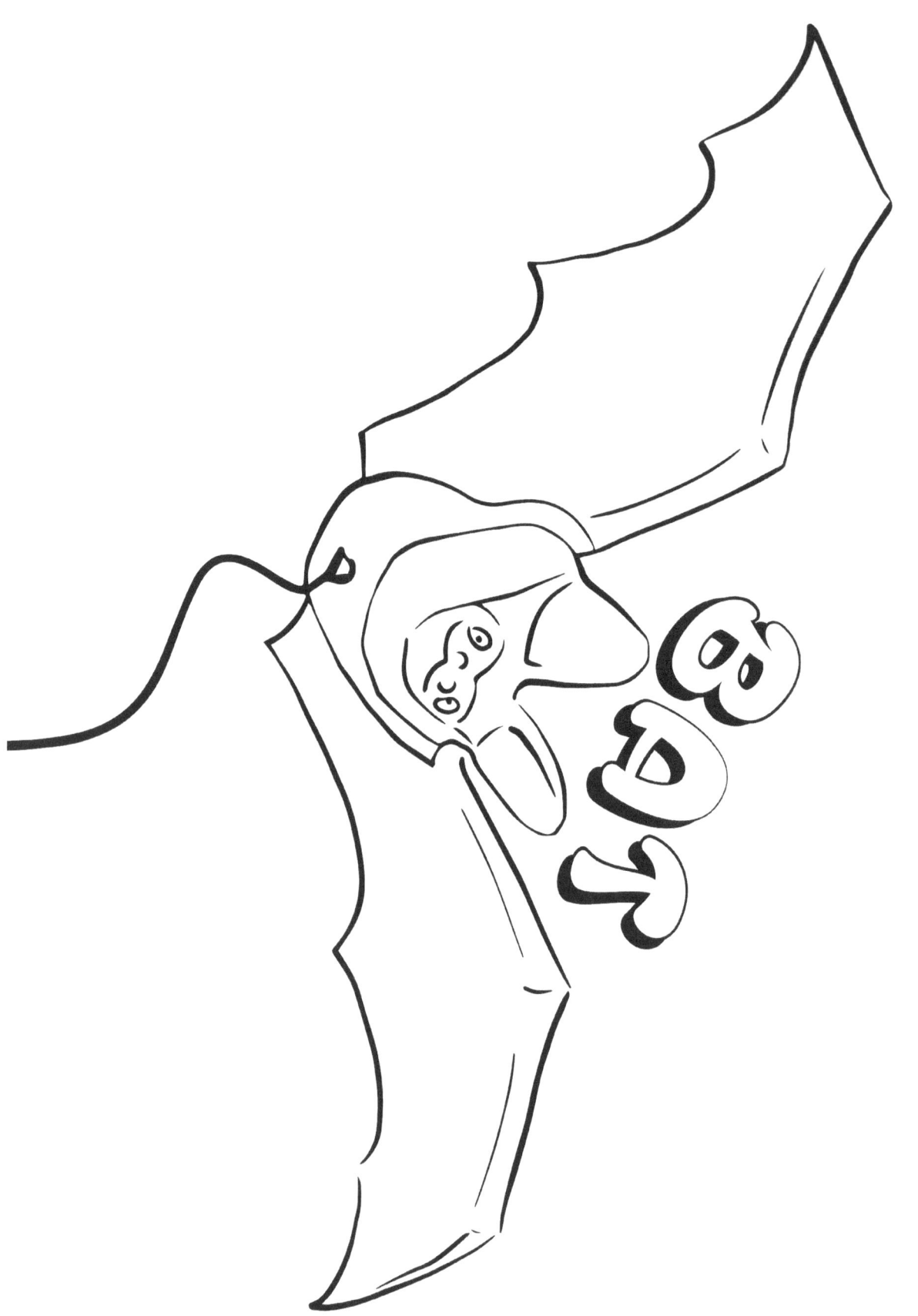

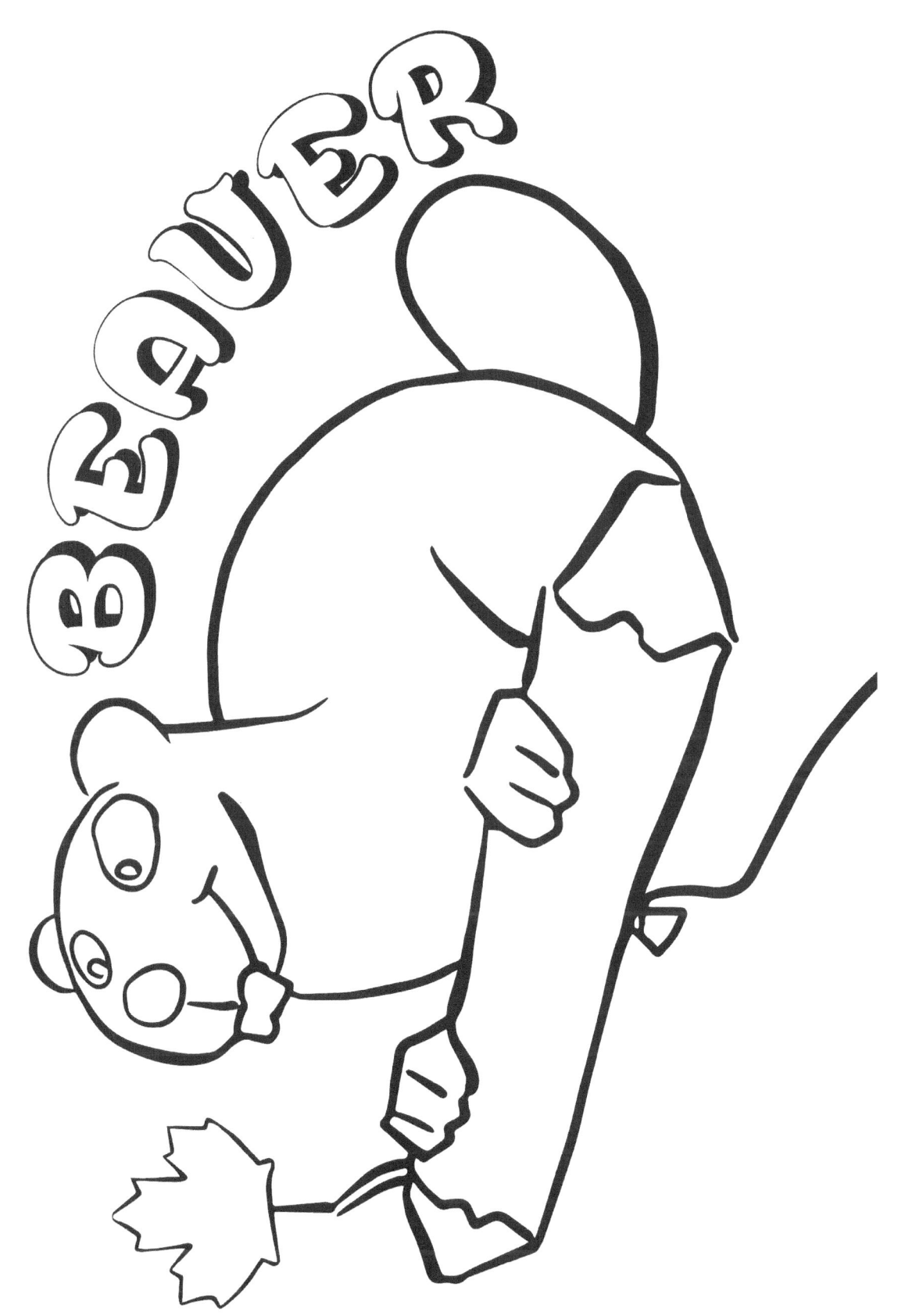

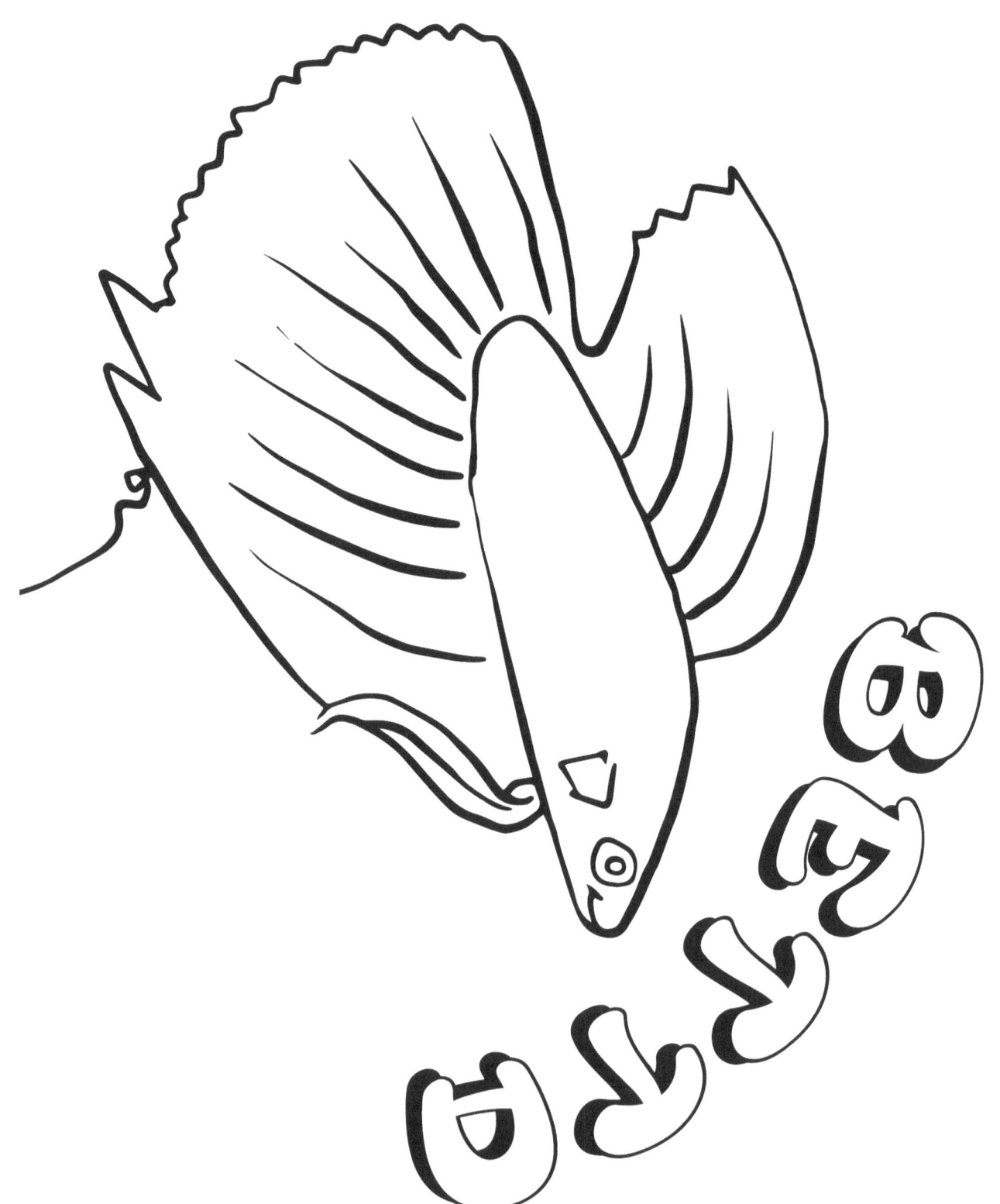

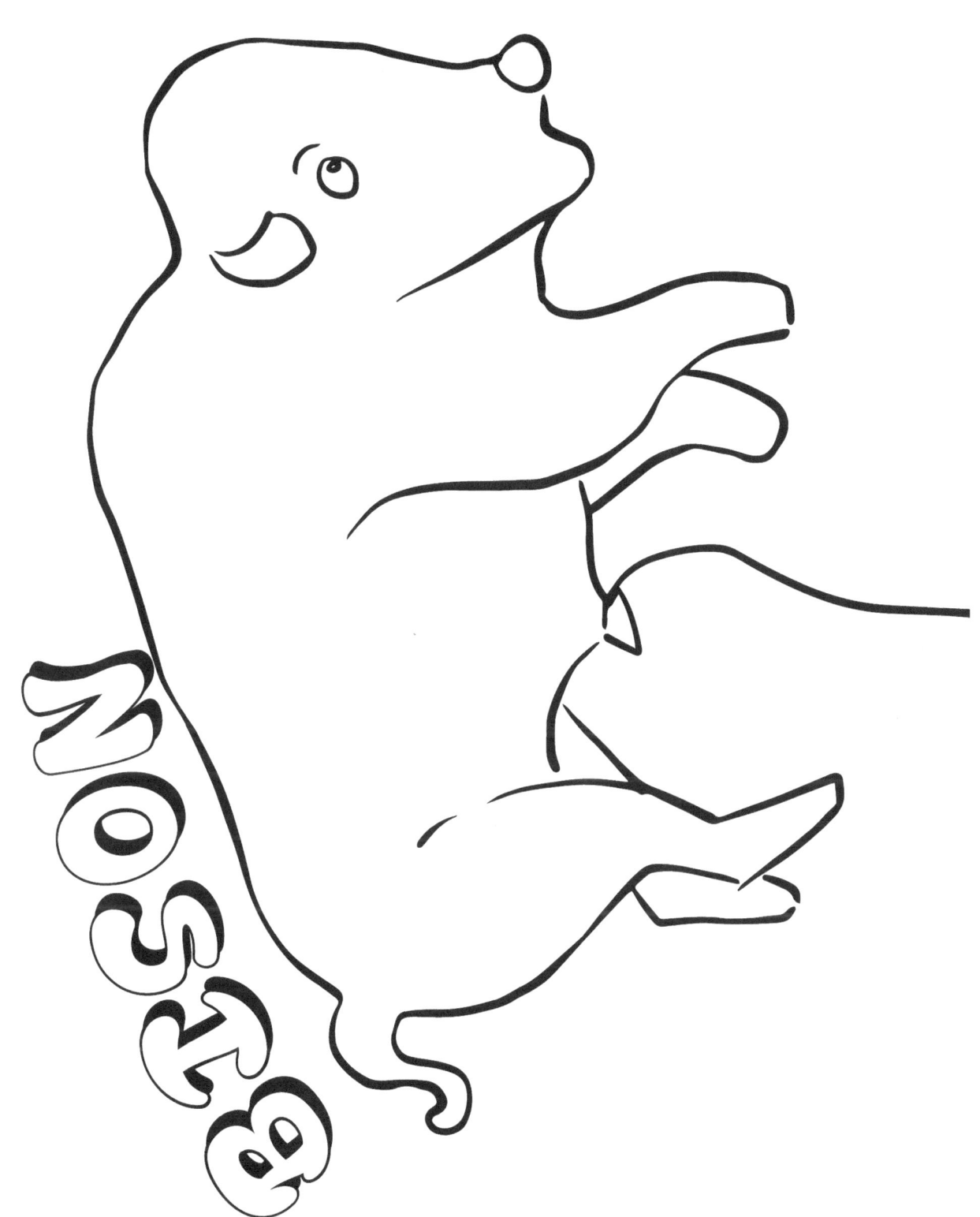

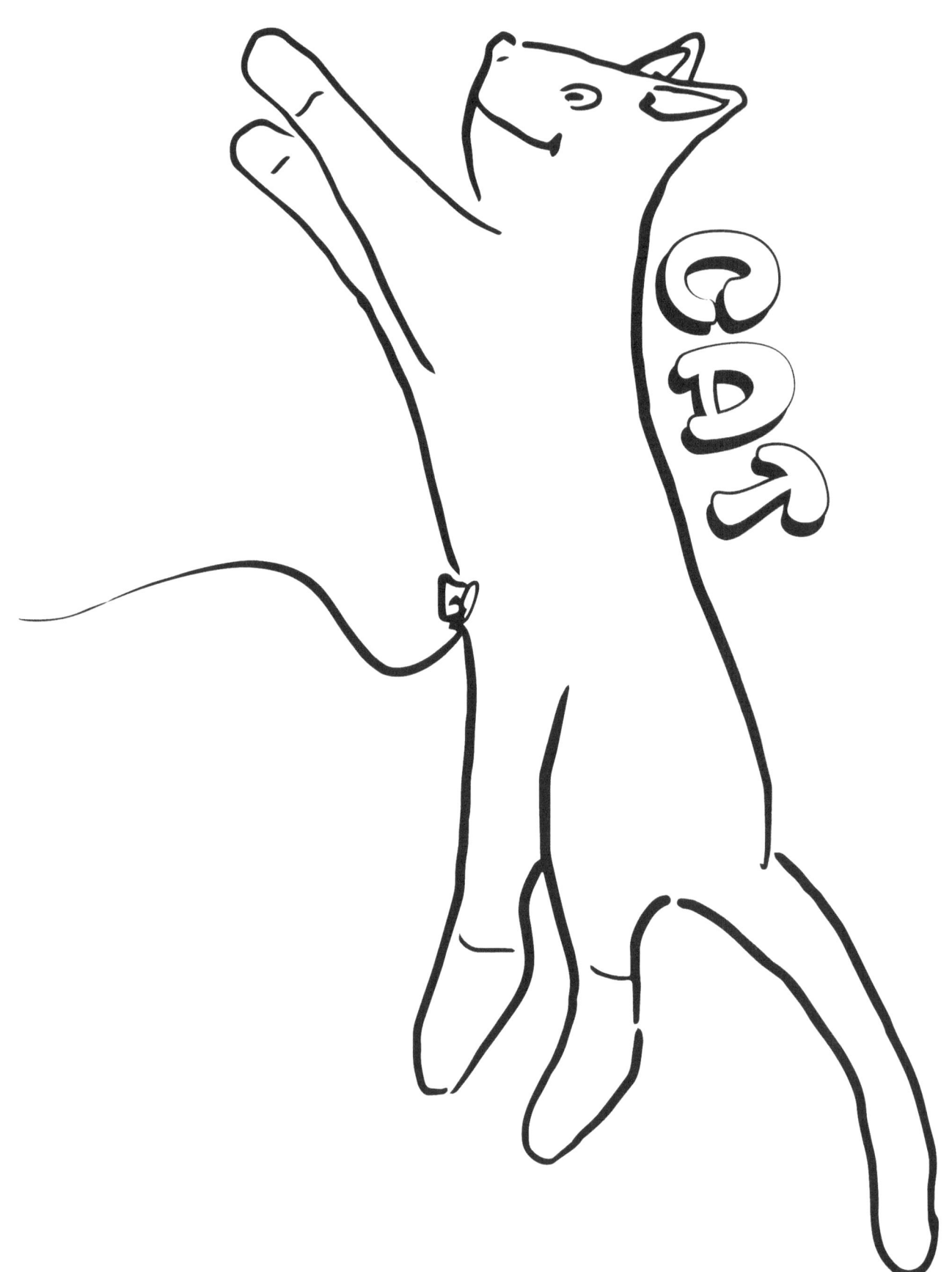

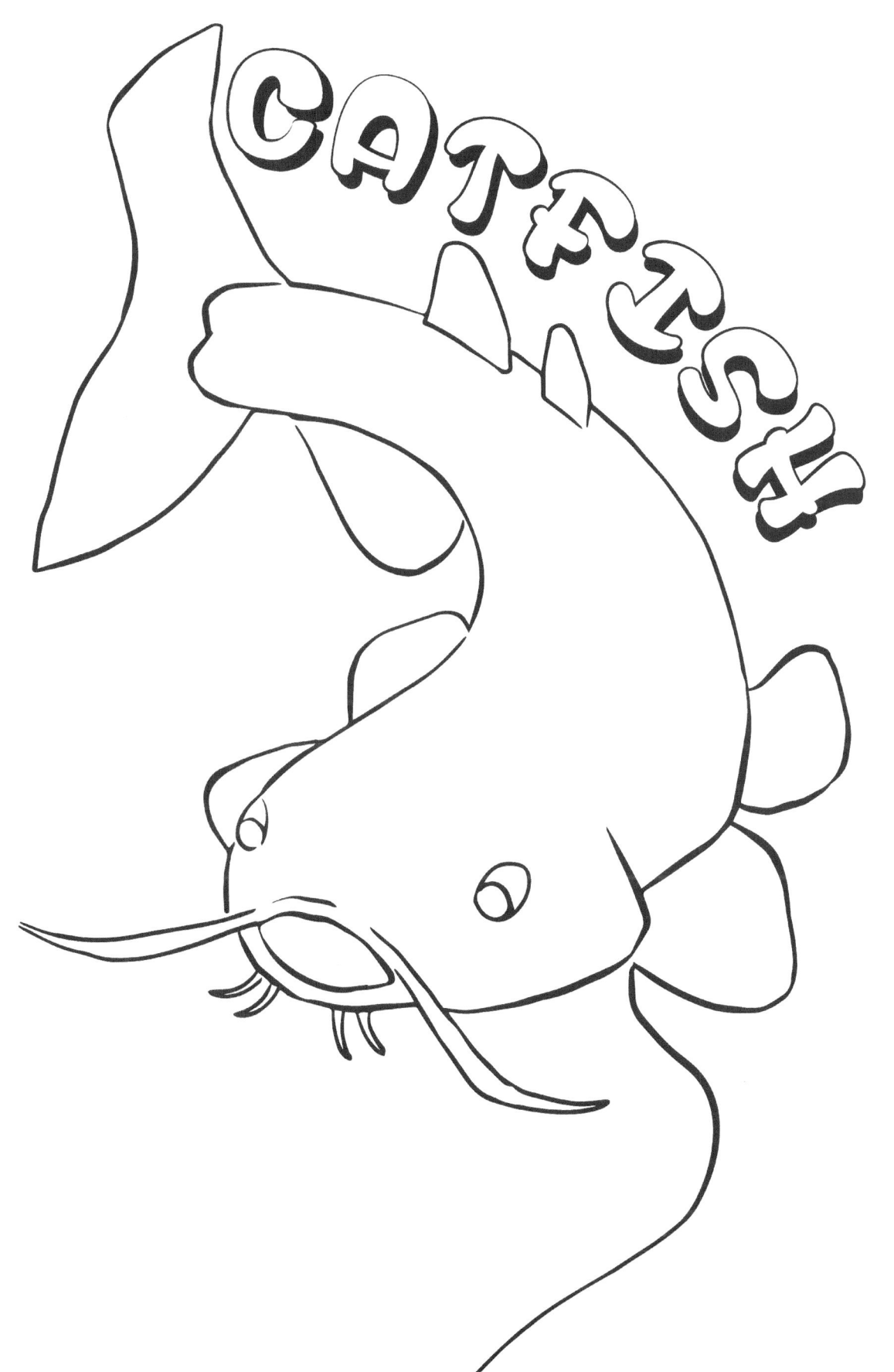

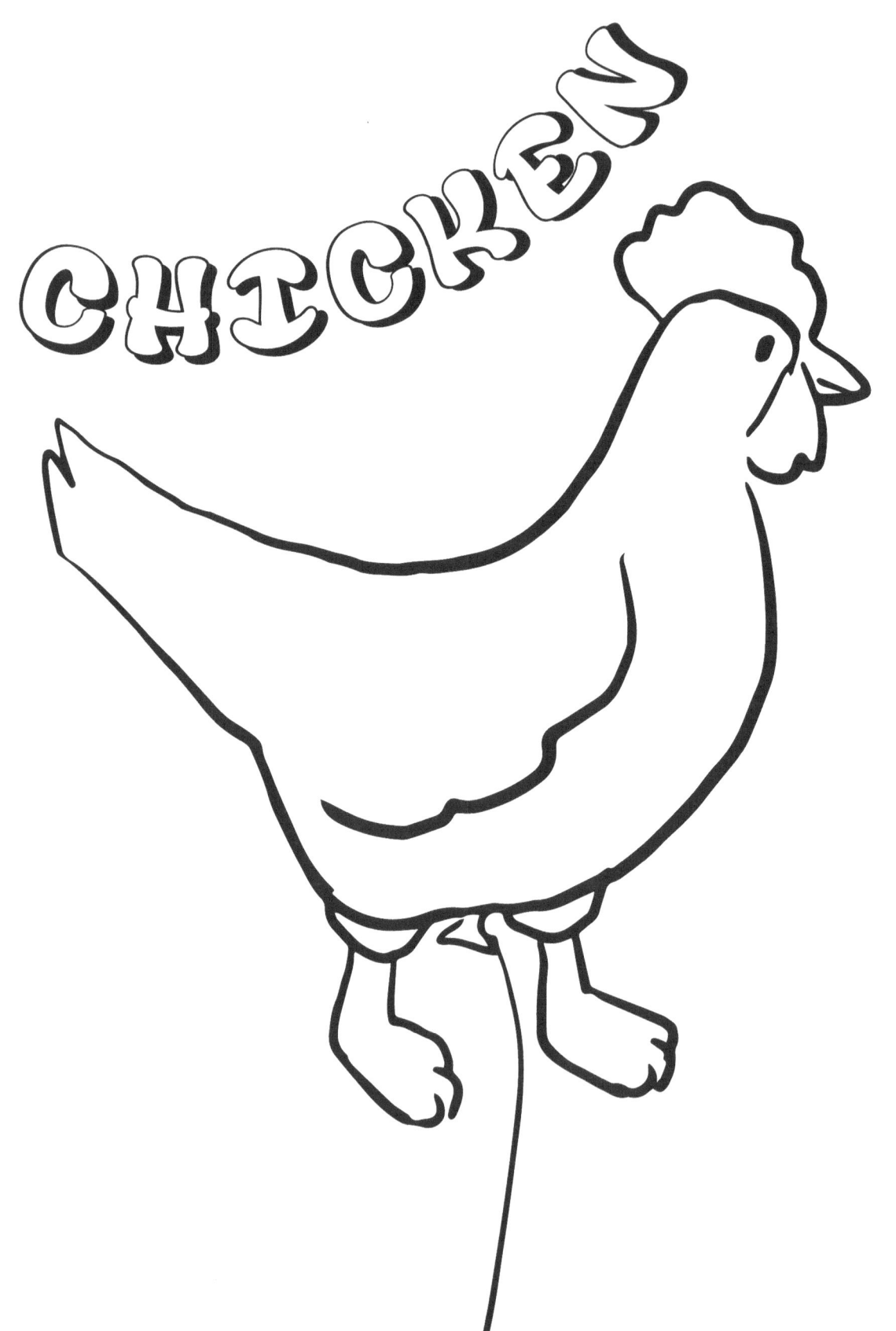

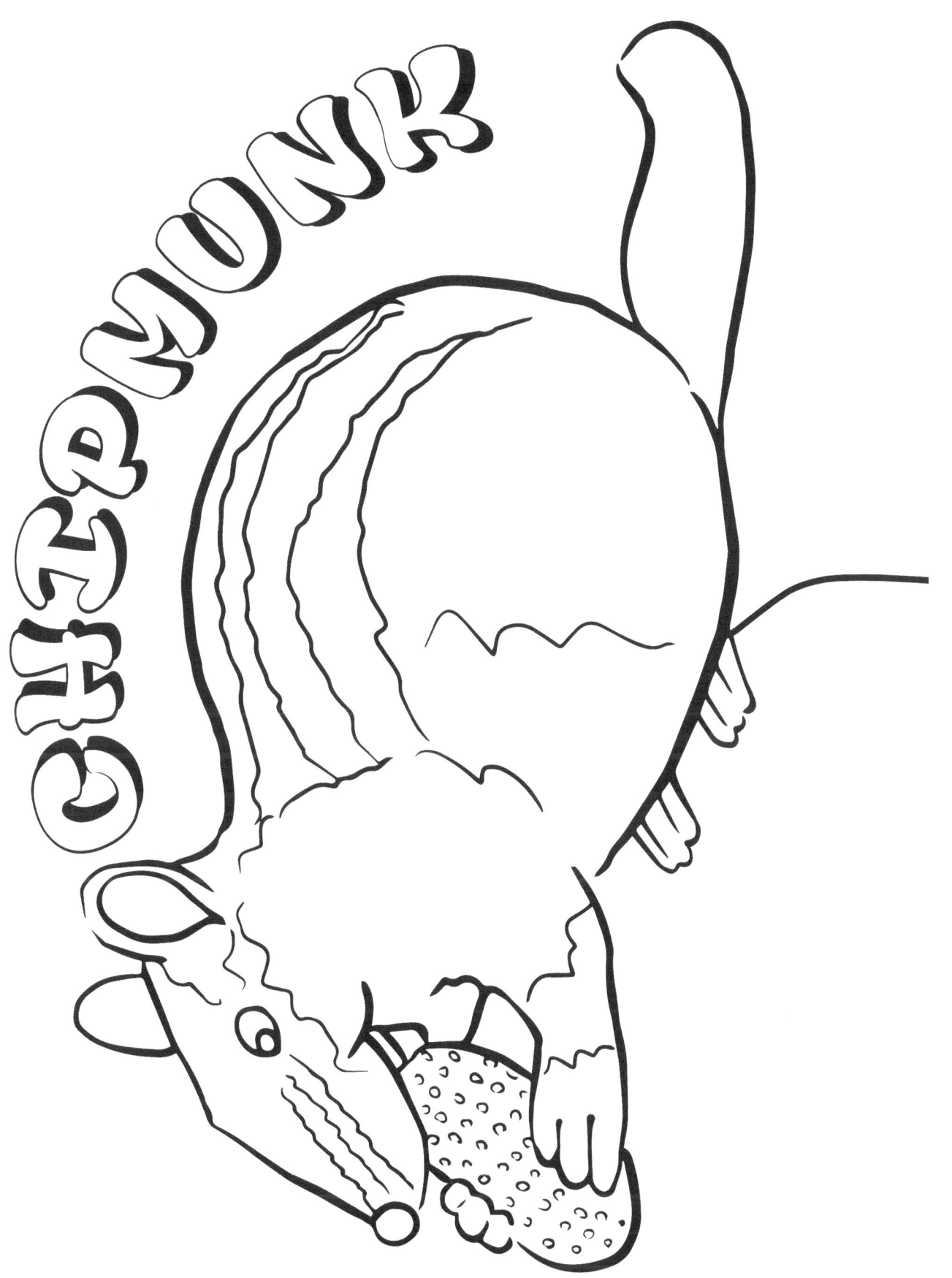

CHIPMUNK

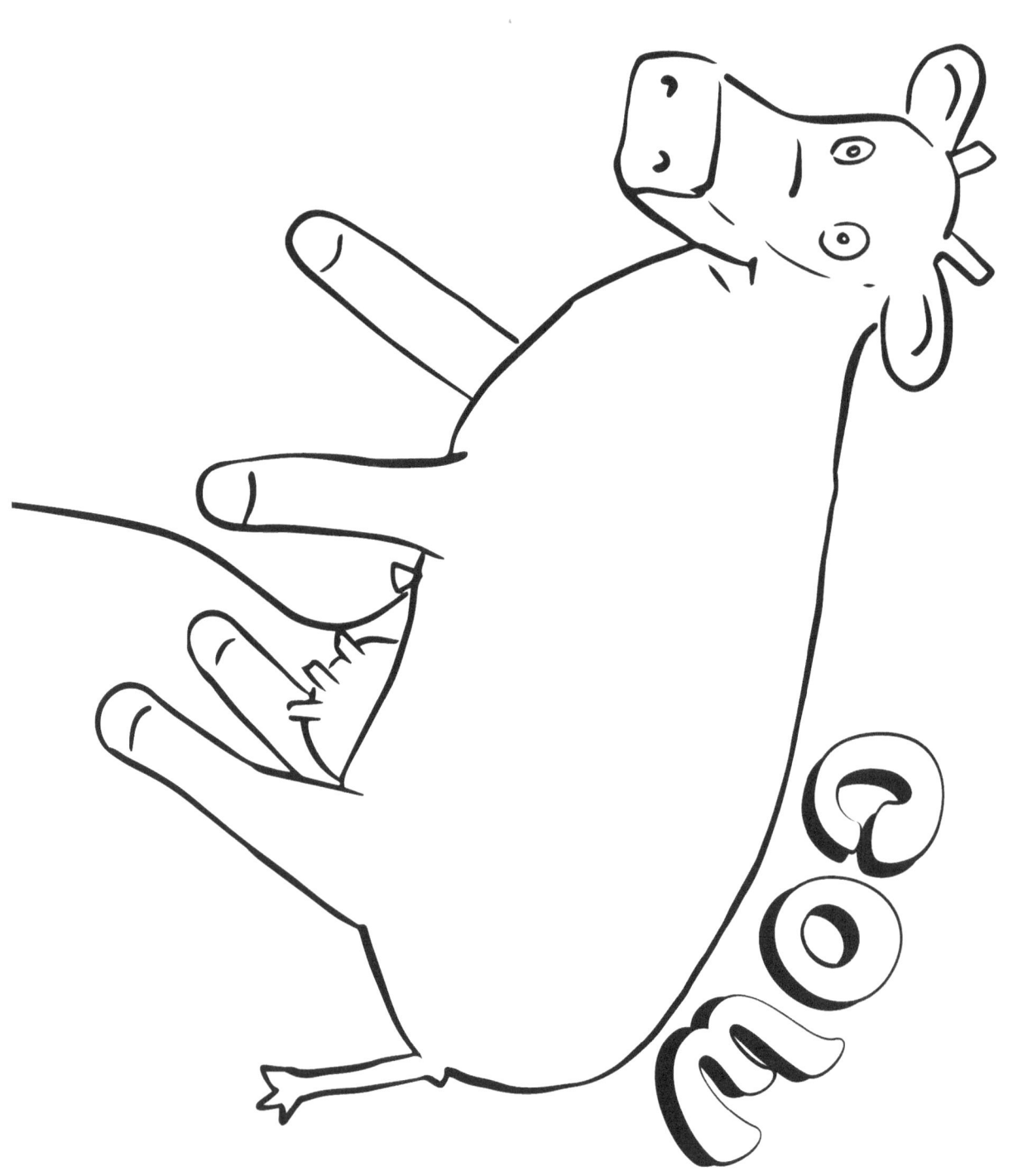

cow

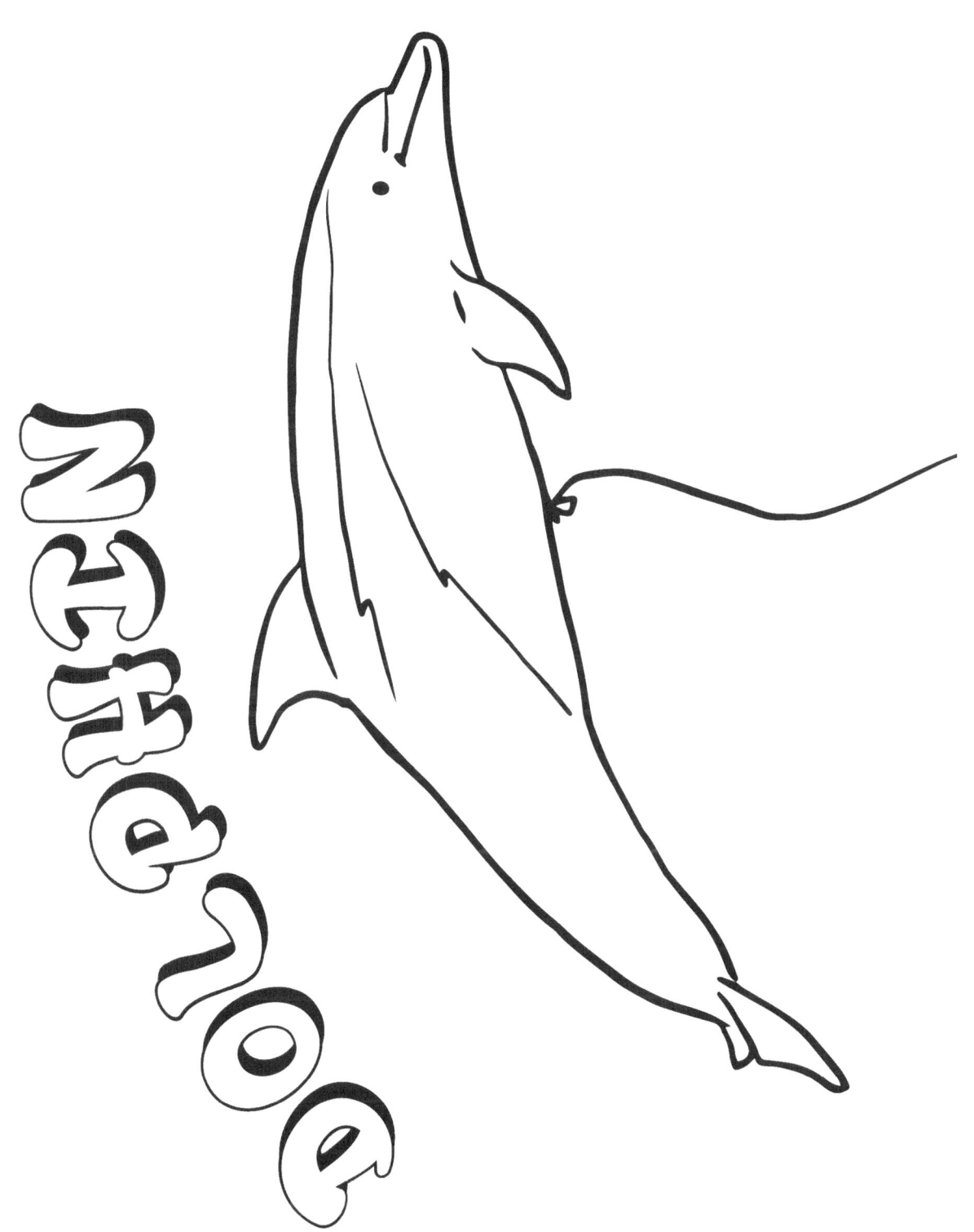

DOLPHIN

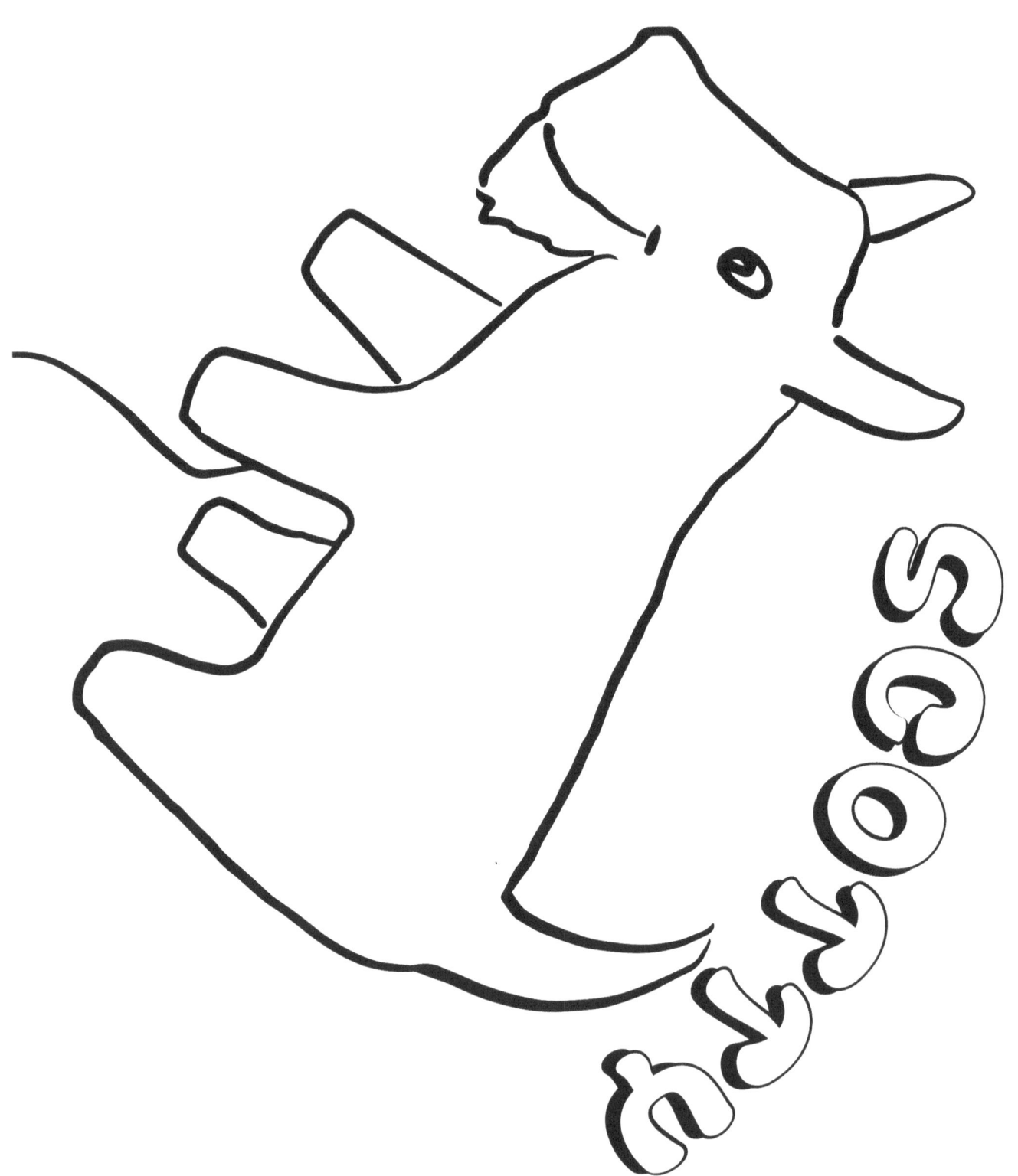

scorry

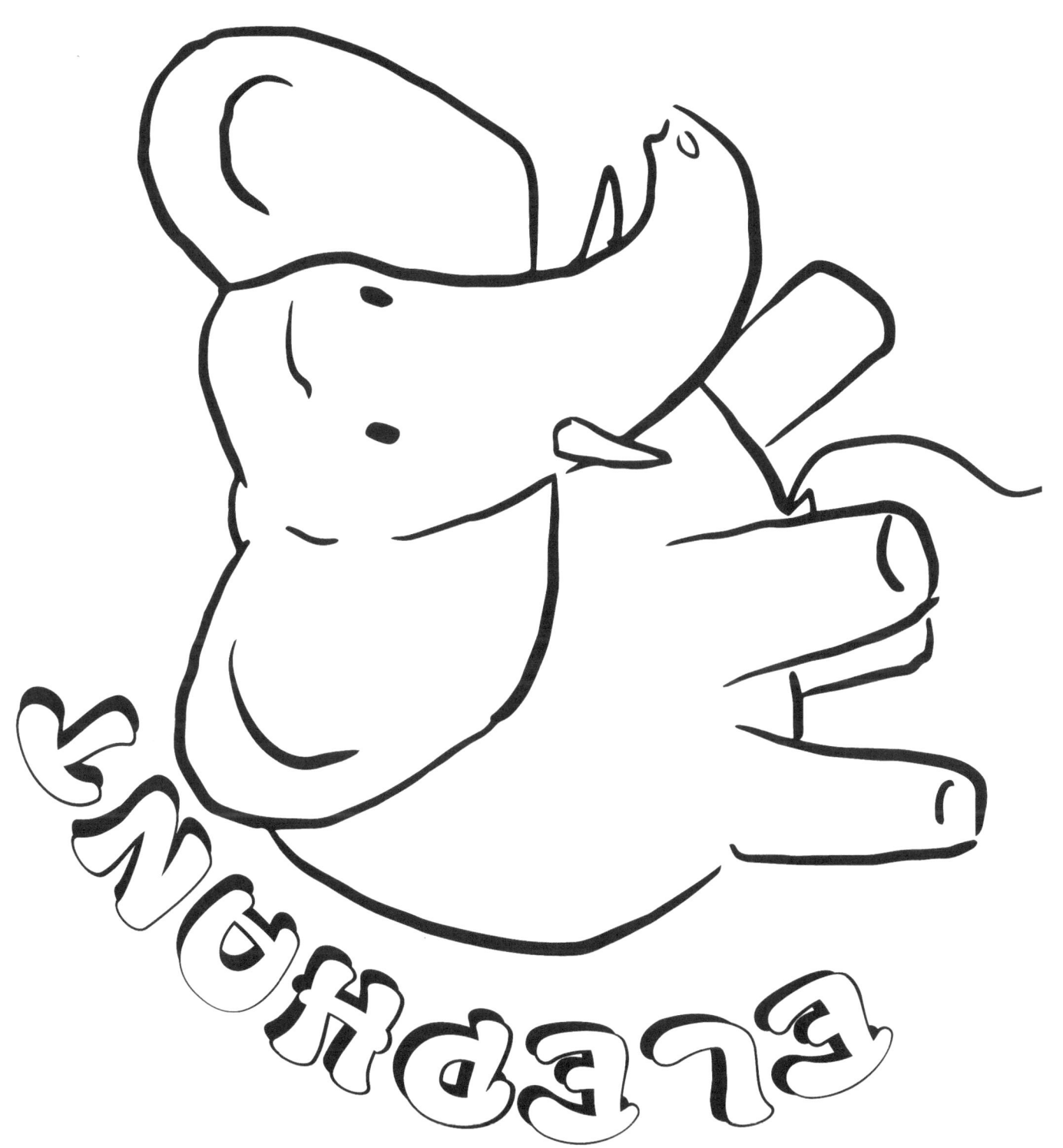

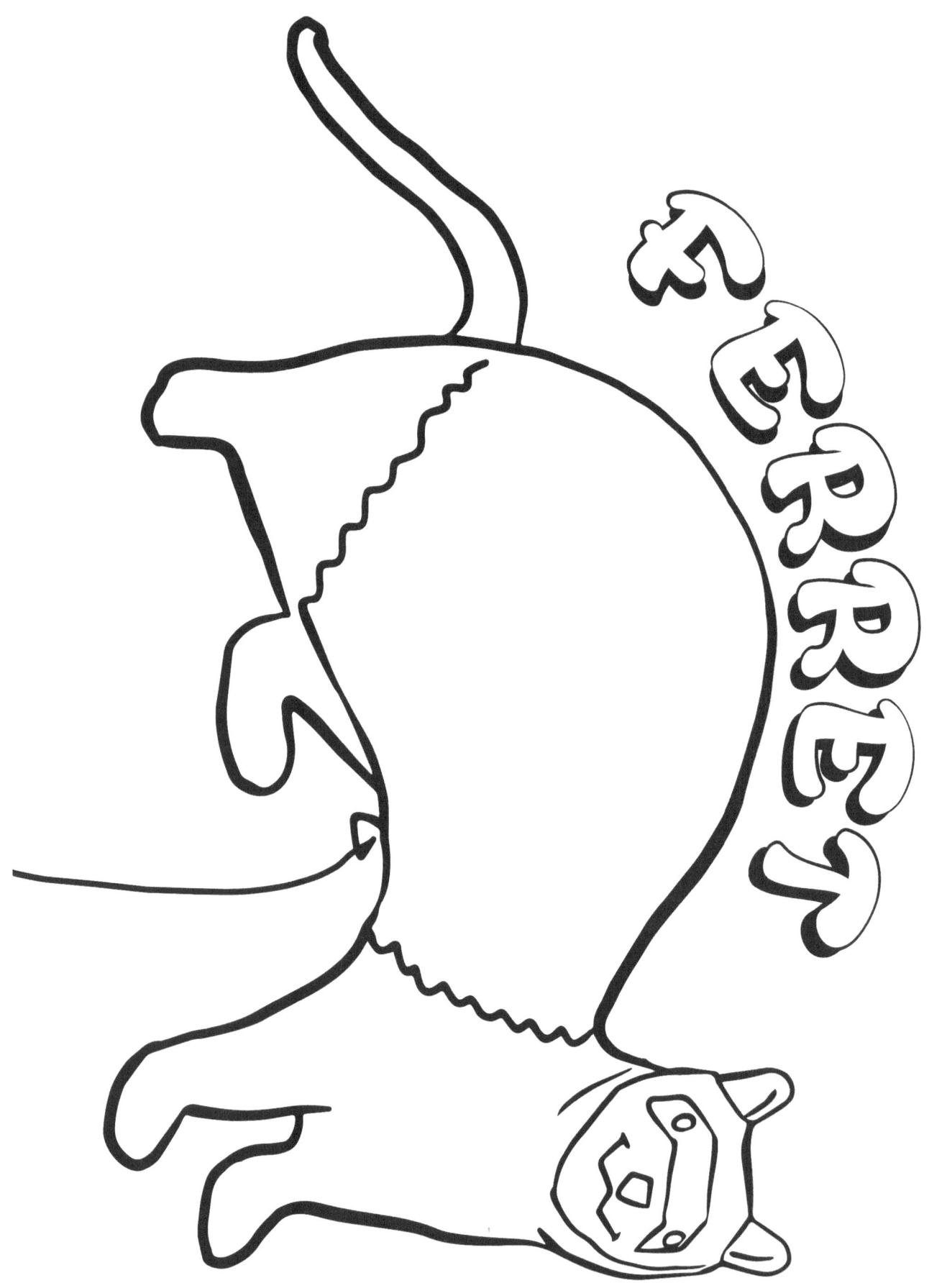

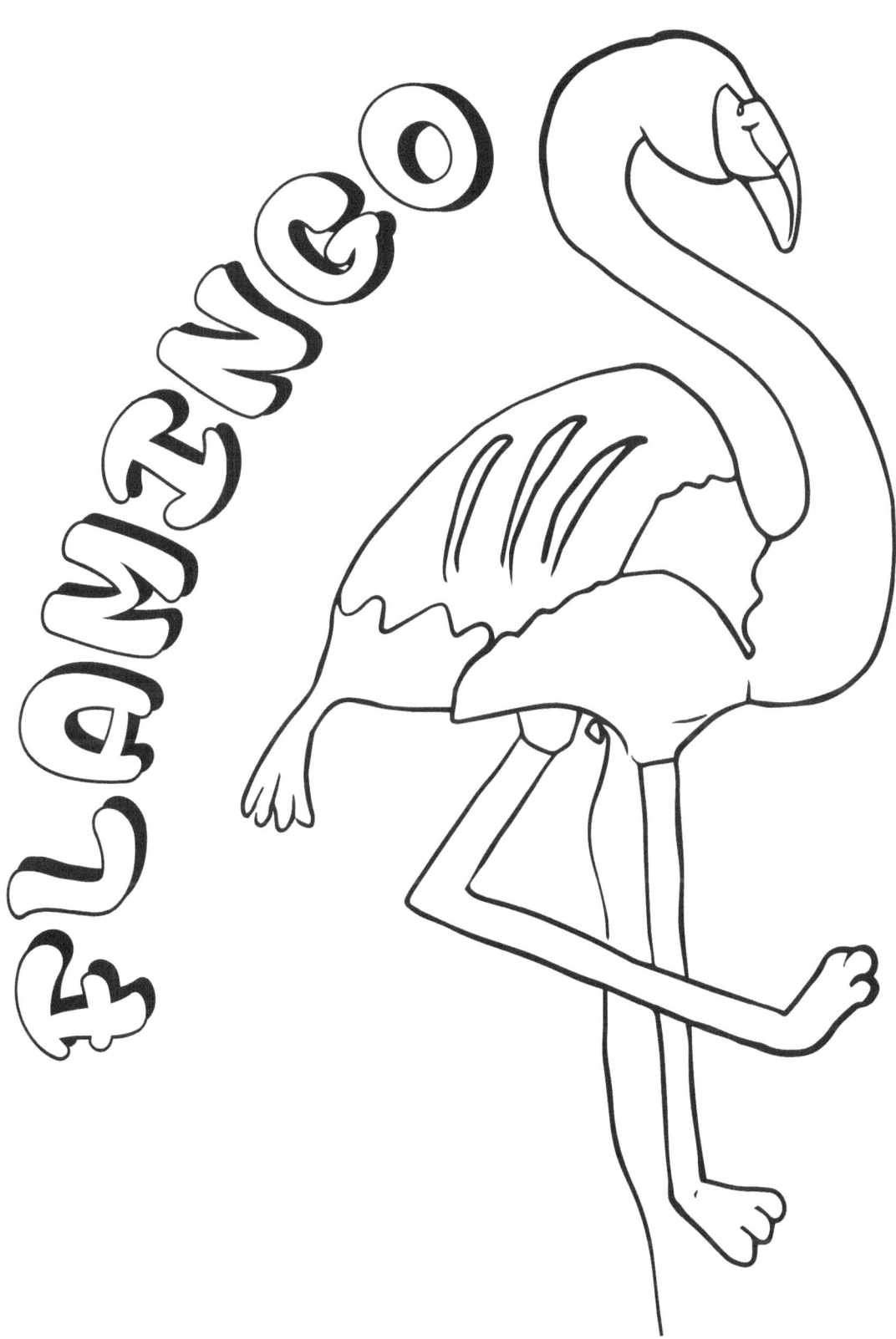

FLAMINGO

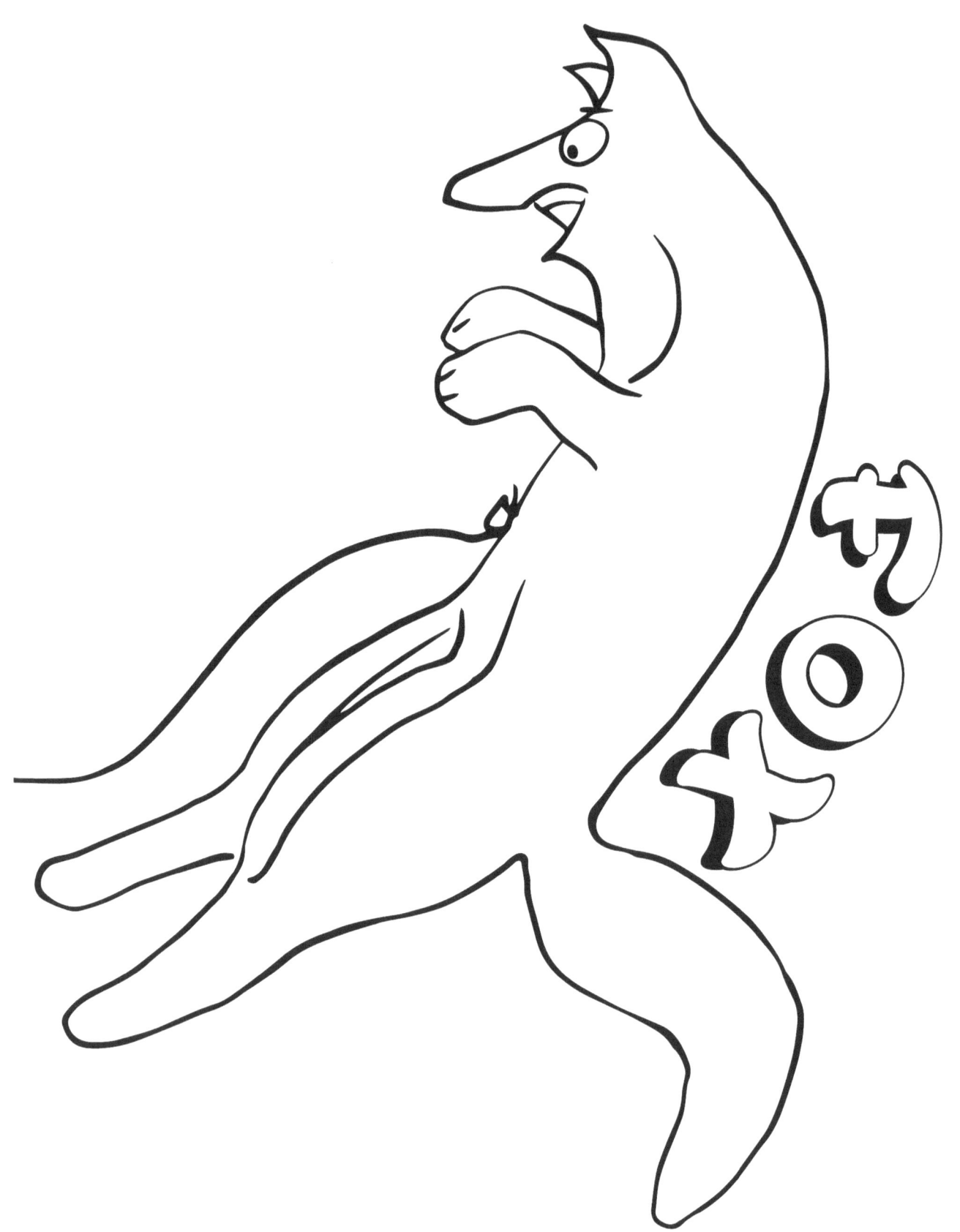

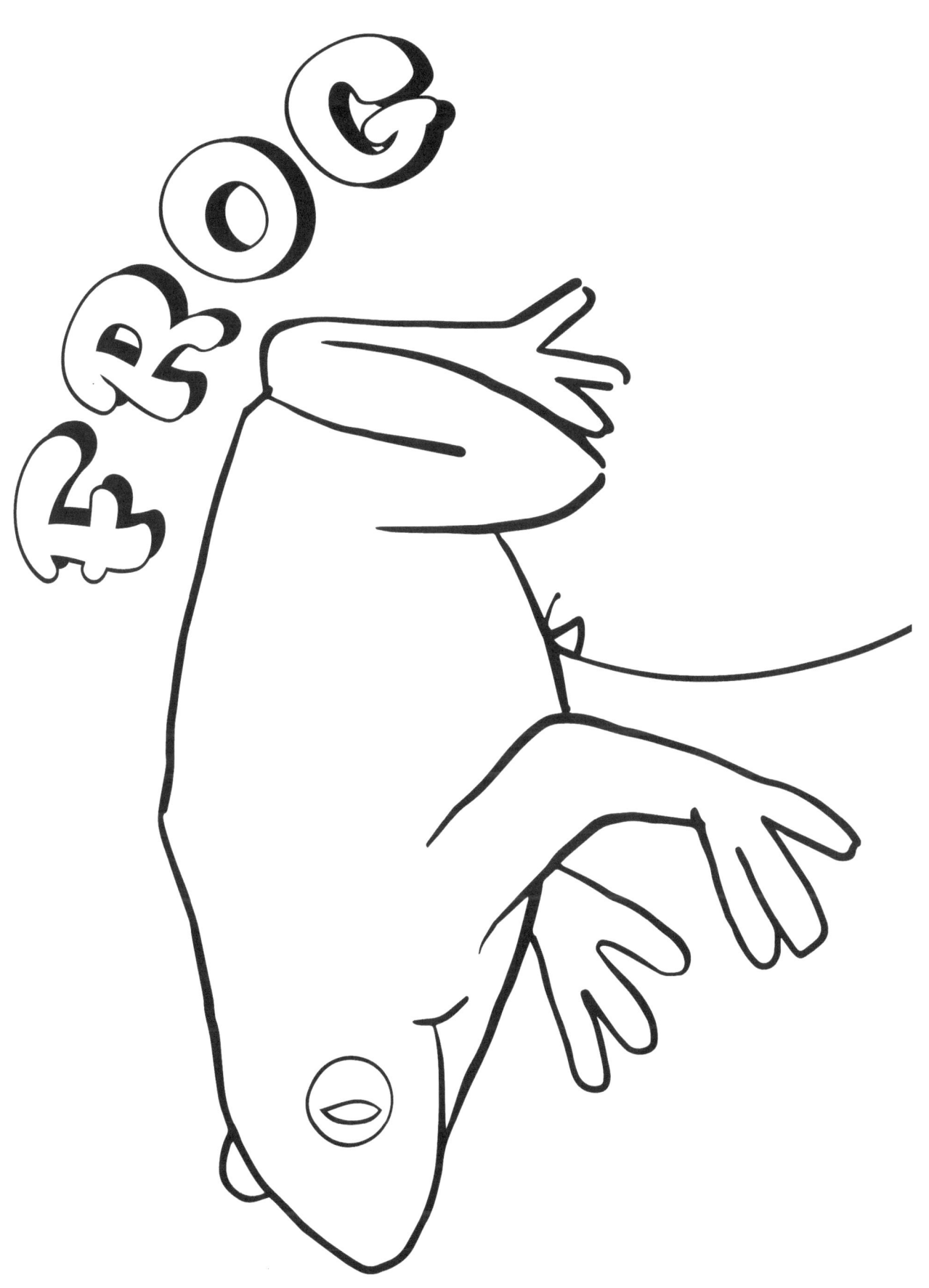

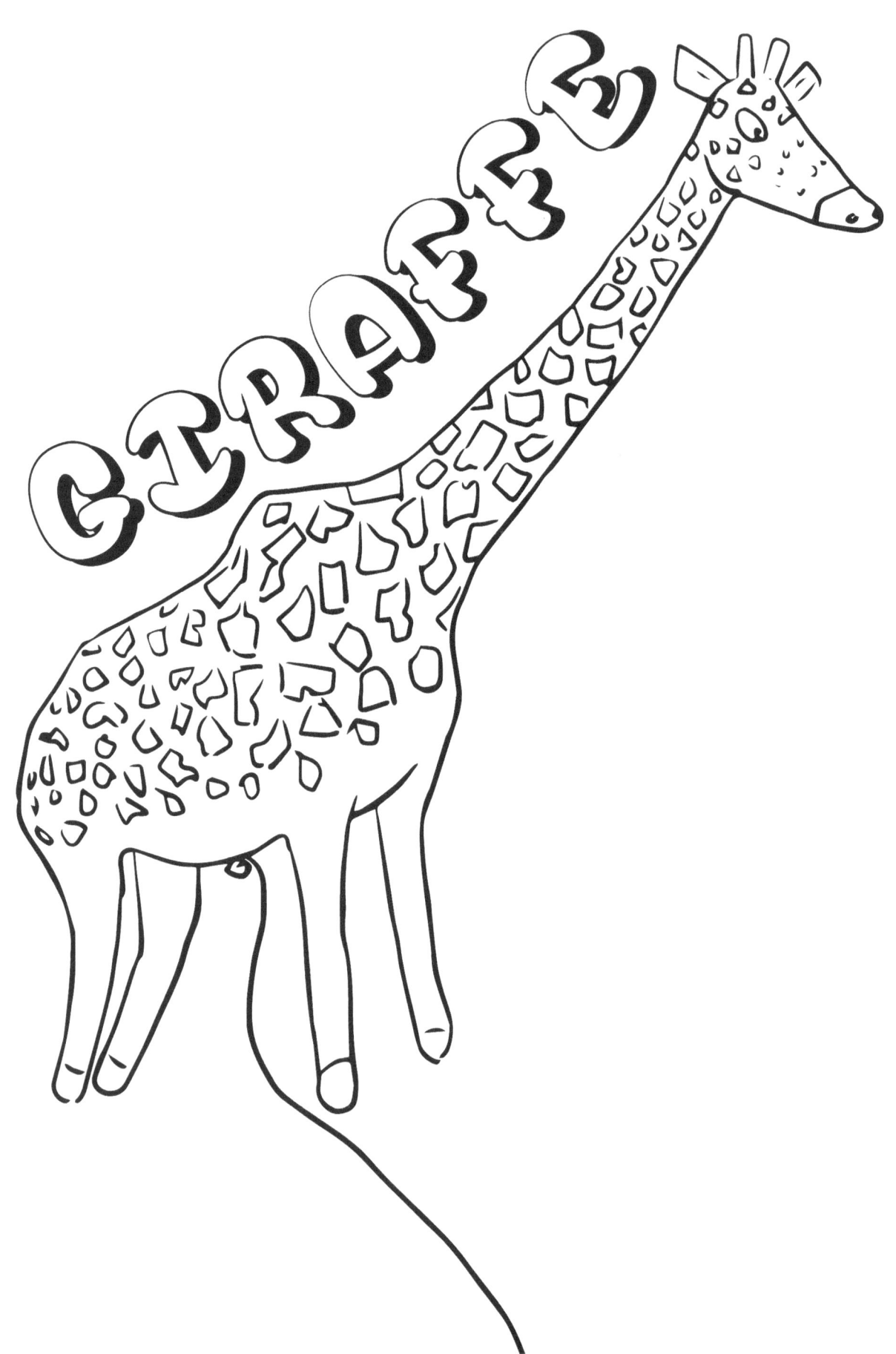

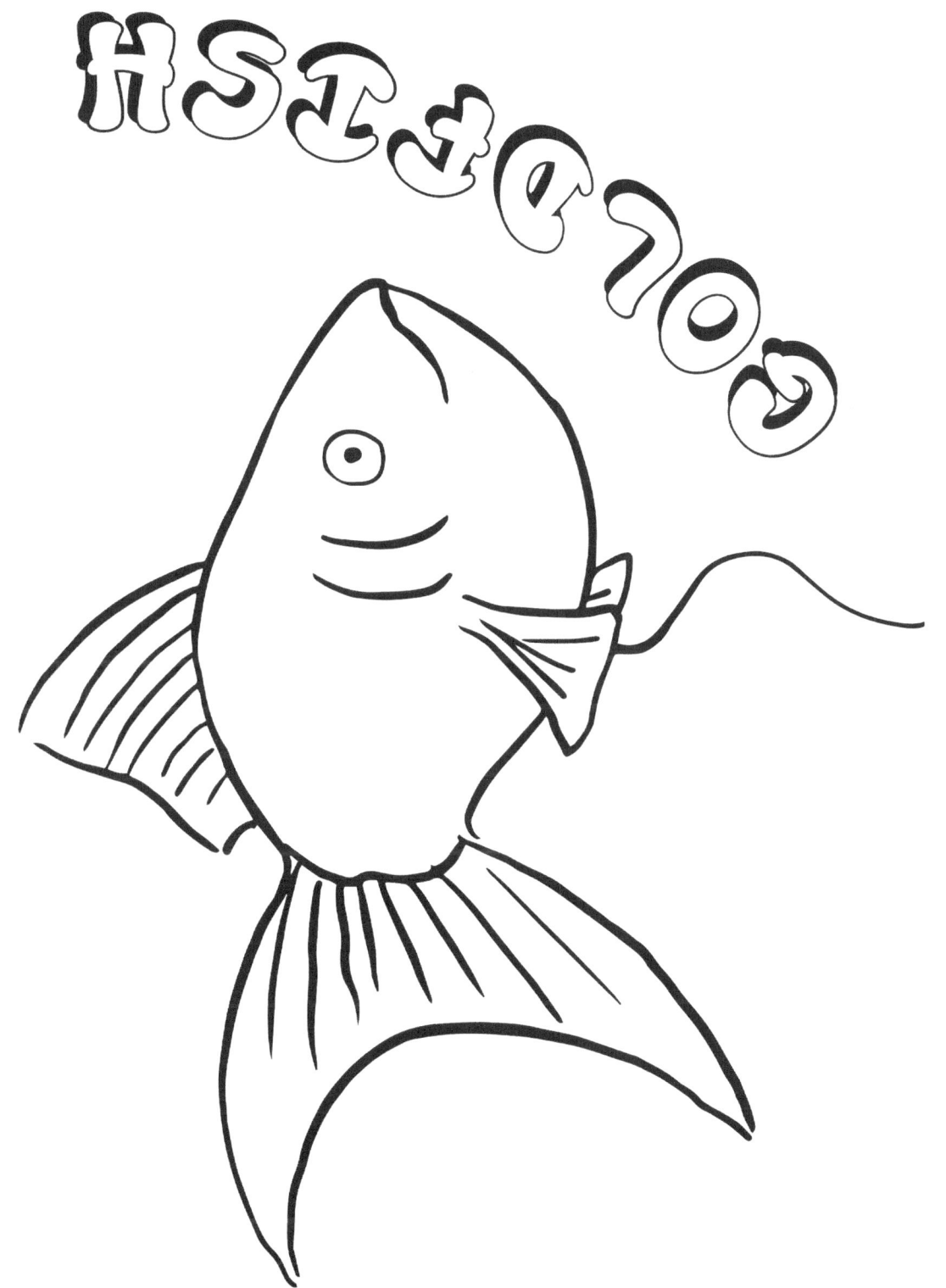

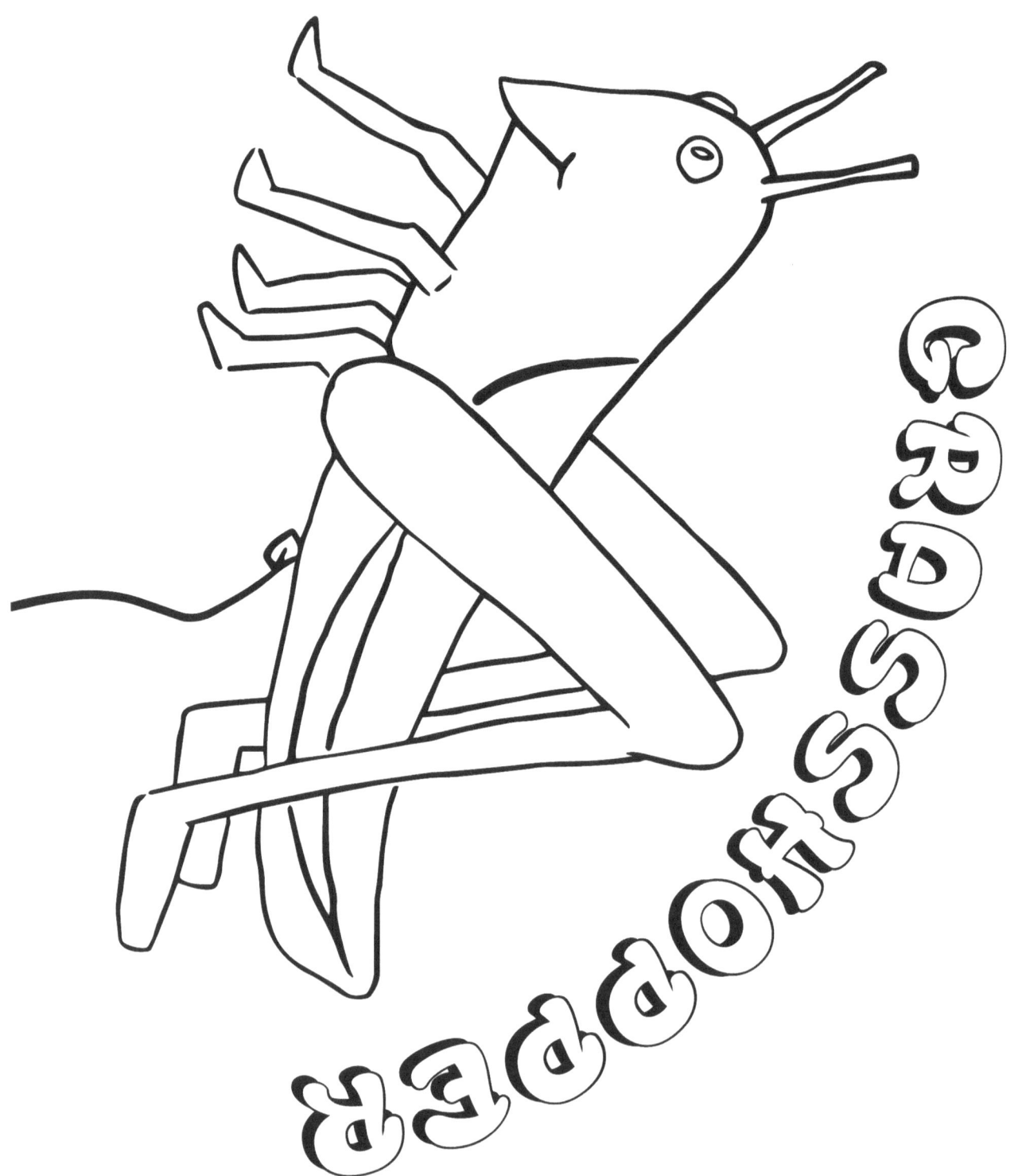

GRASSSHOPPER

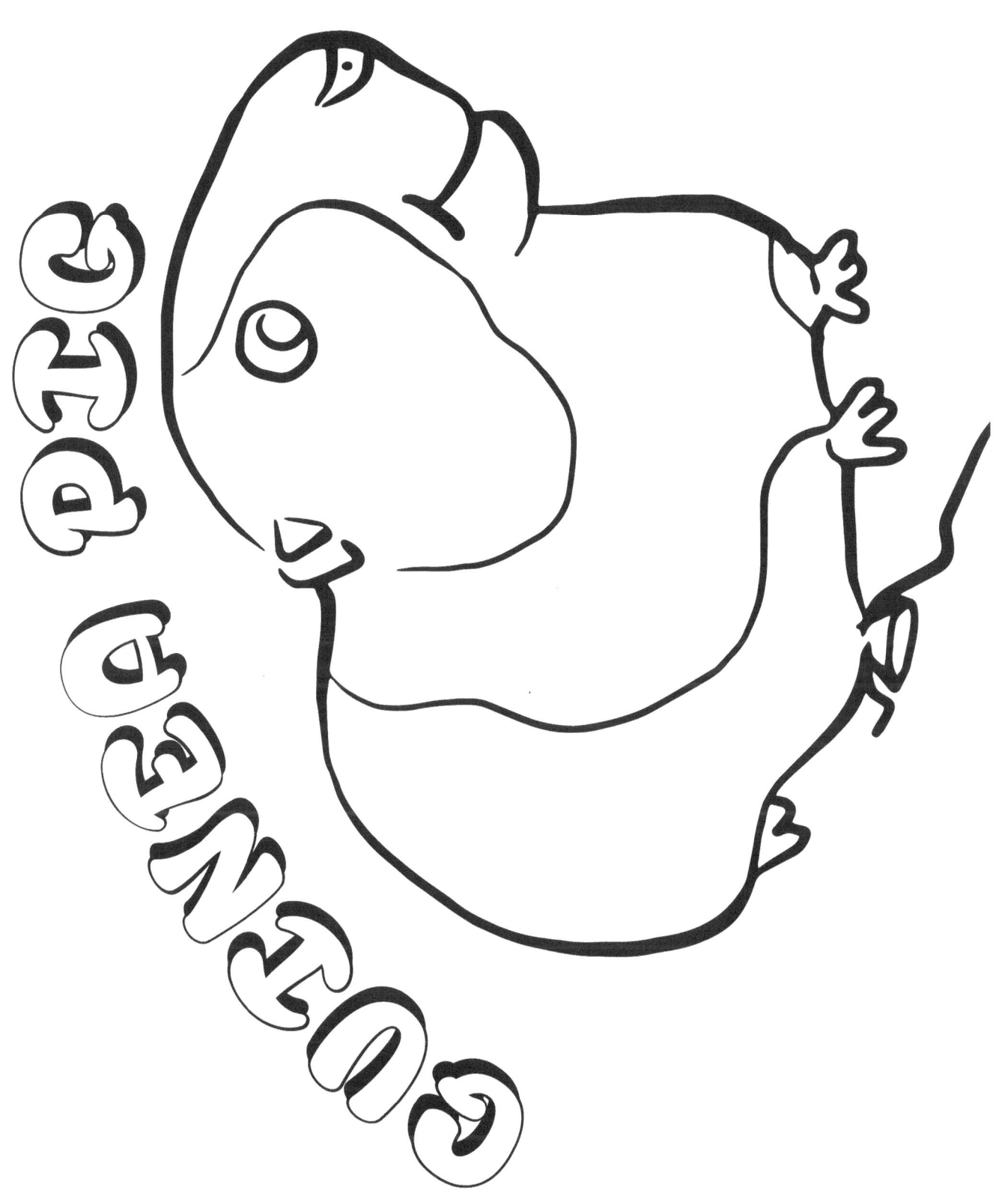

GUINEA PIG

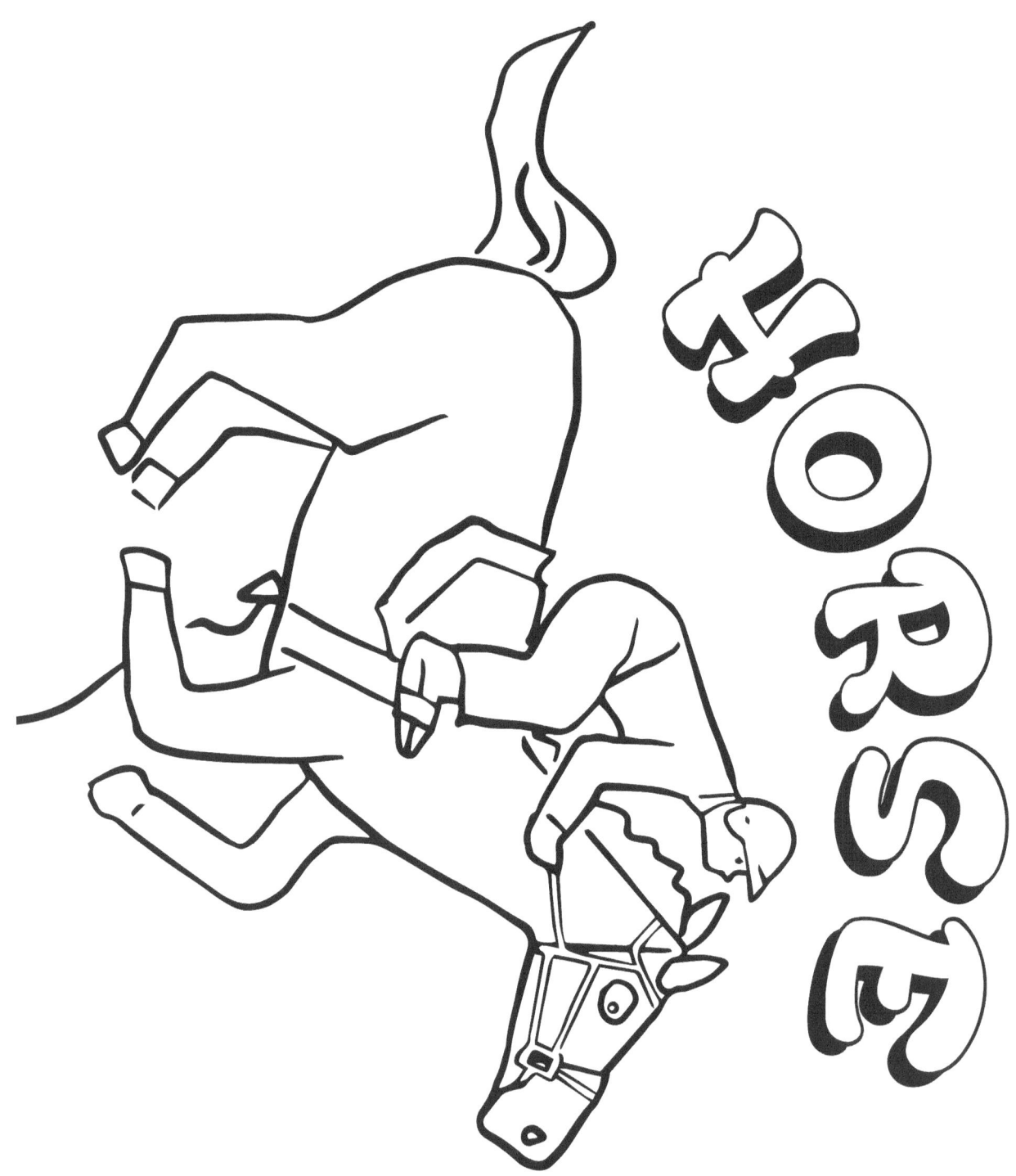

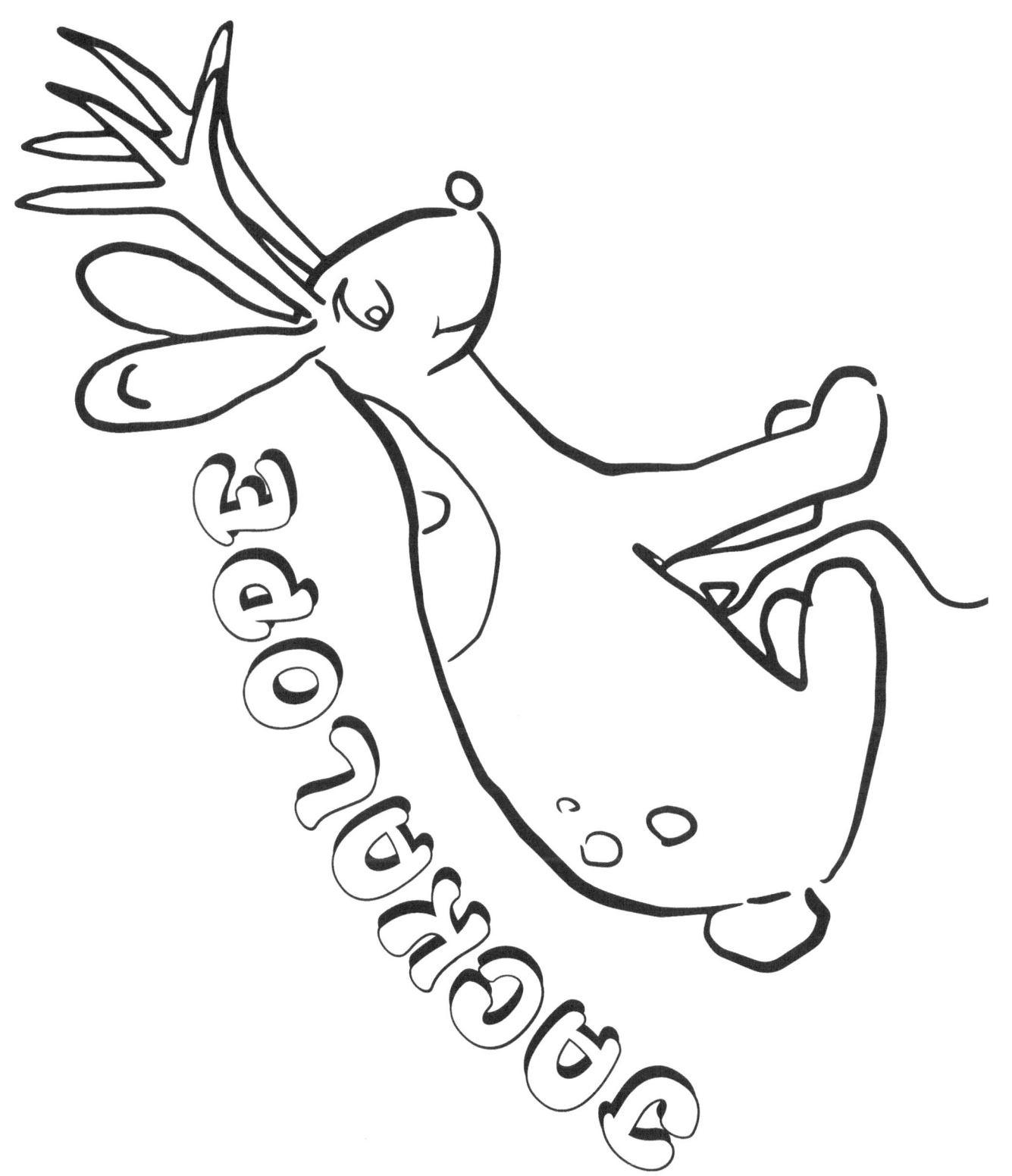

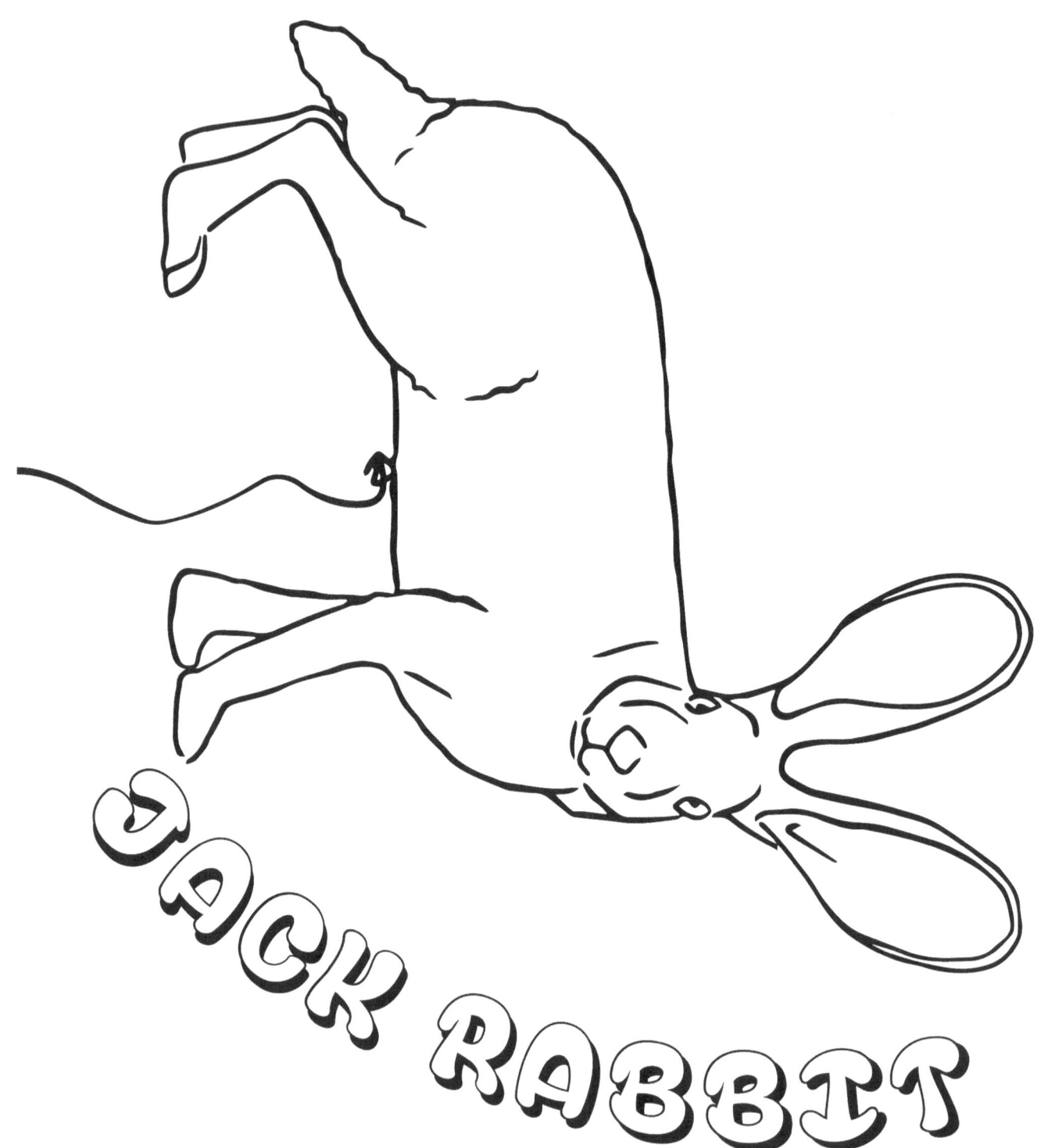

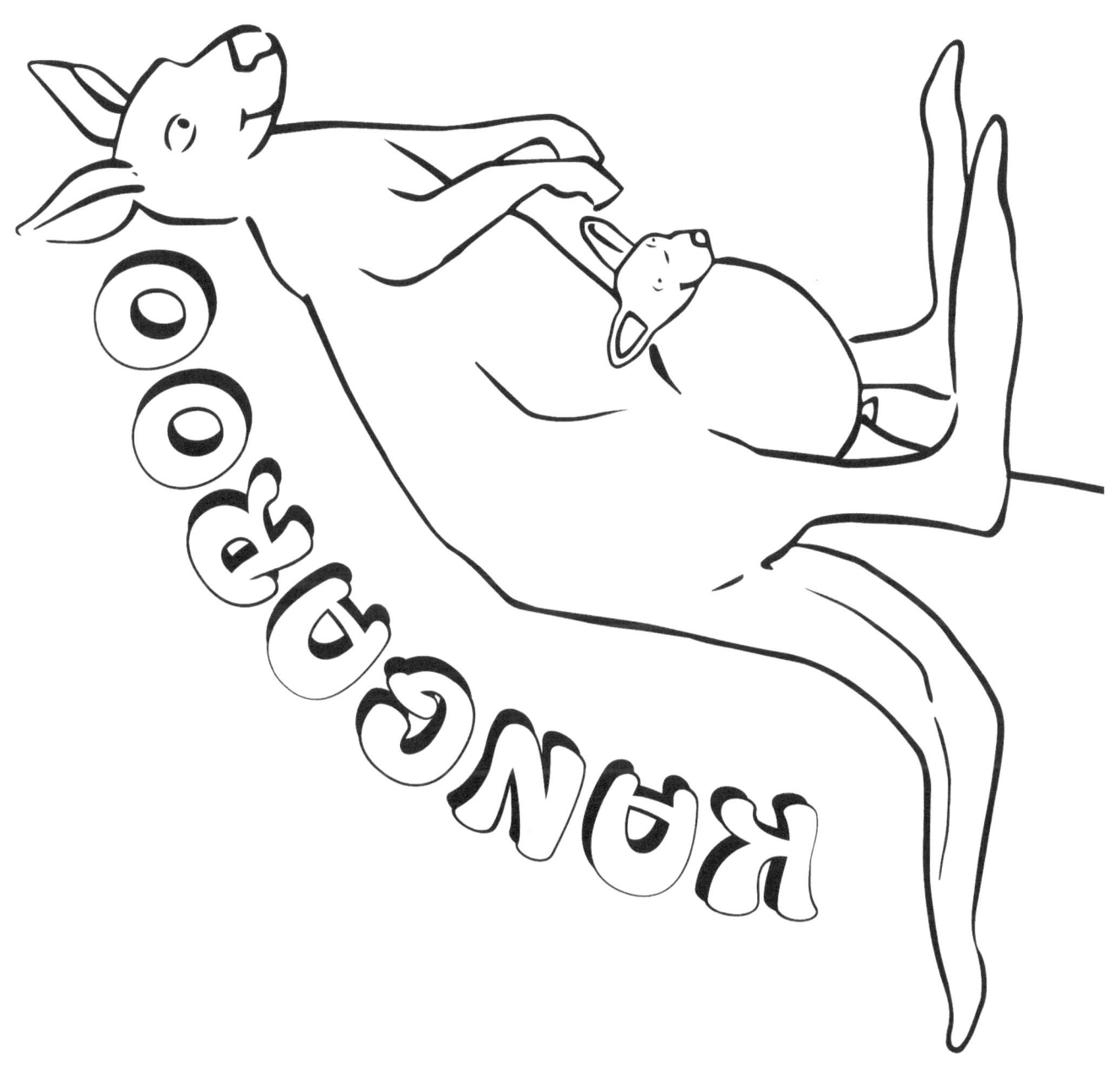

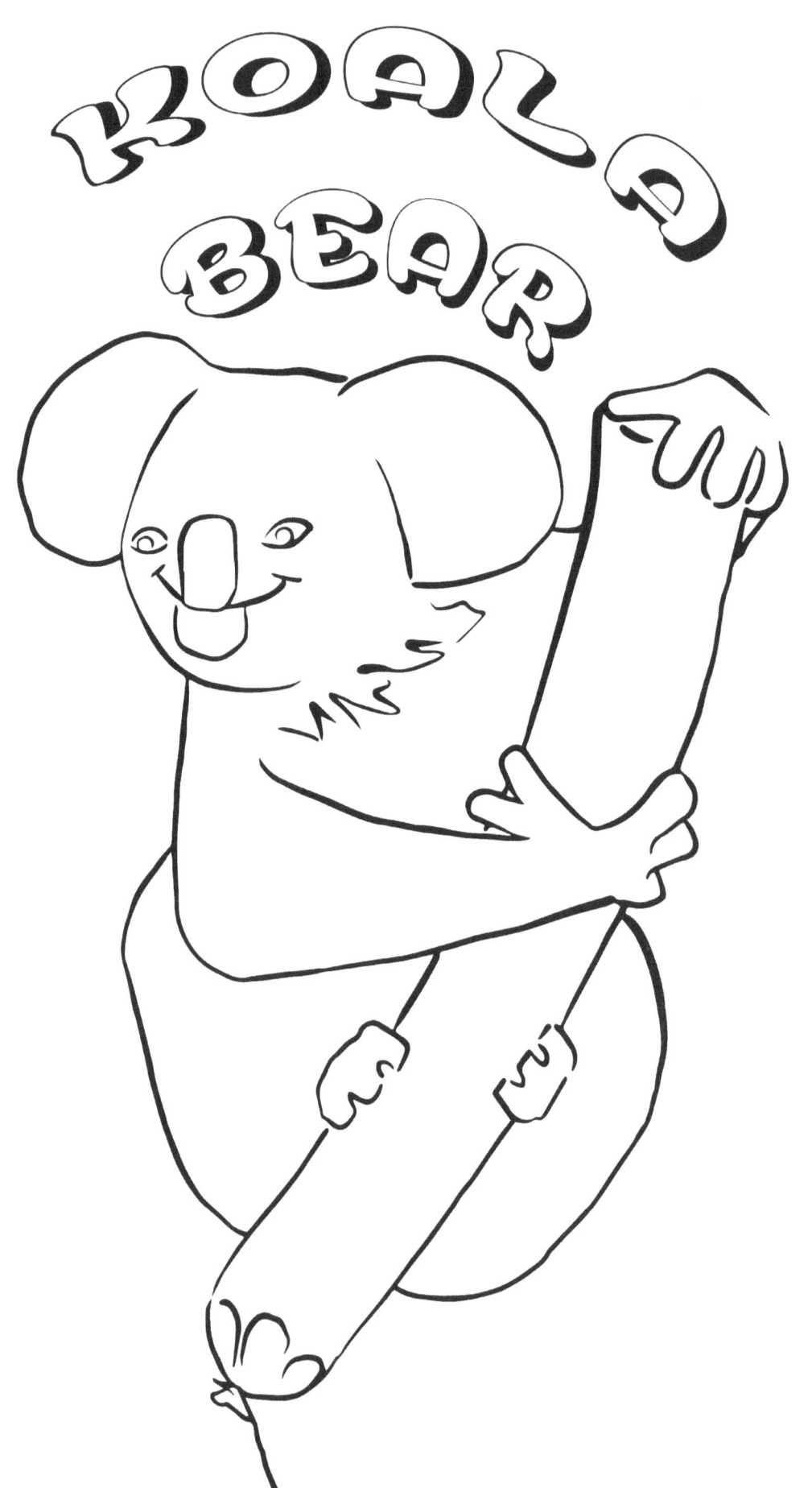

LADY BUG

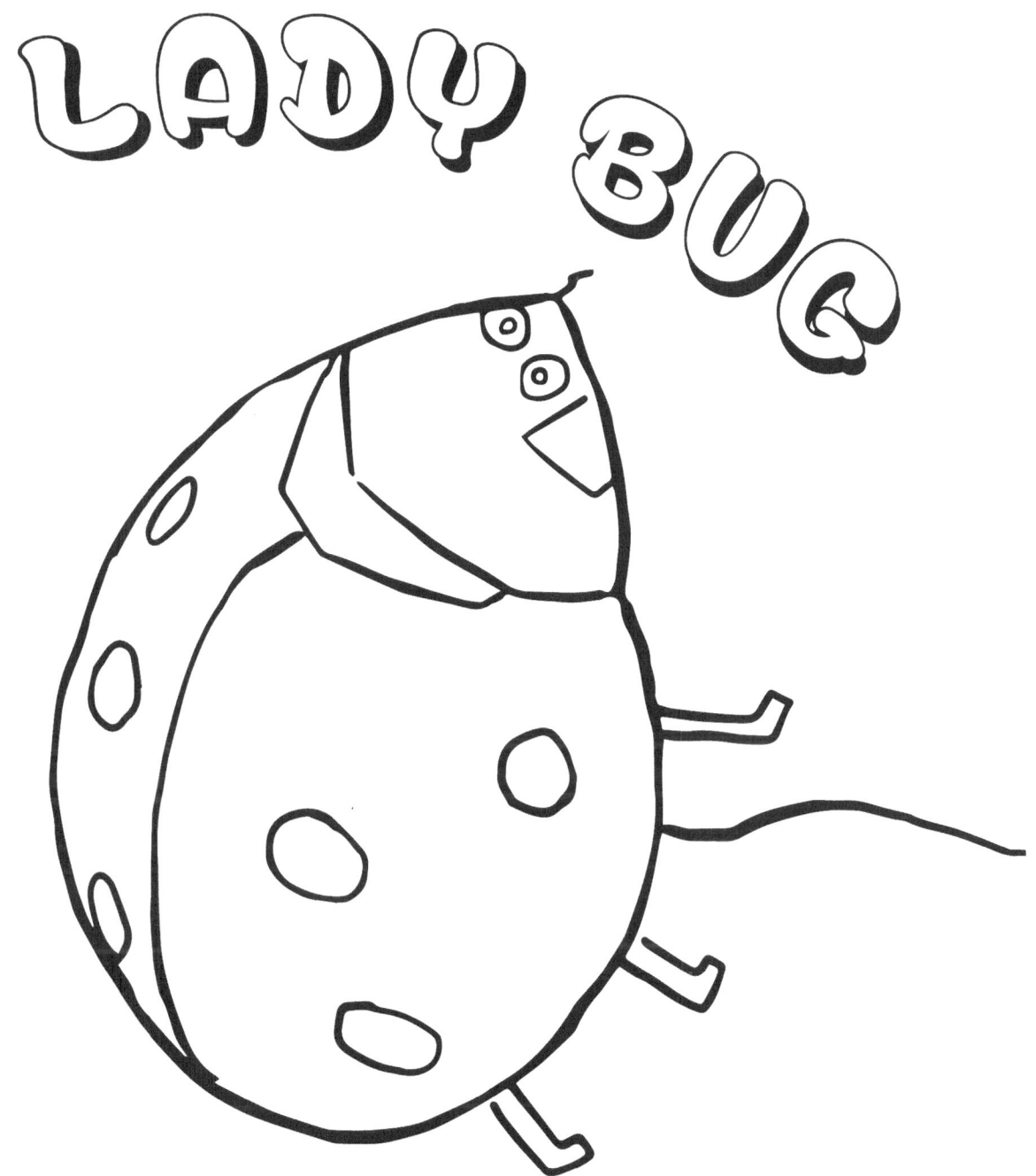

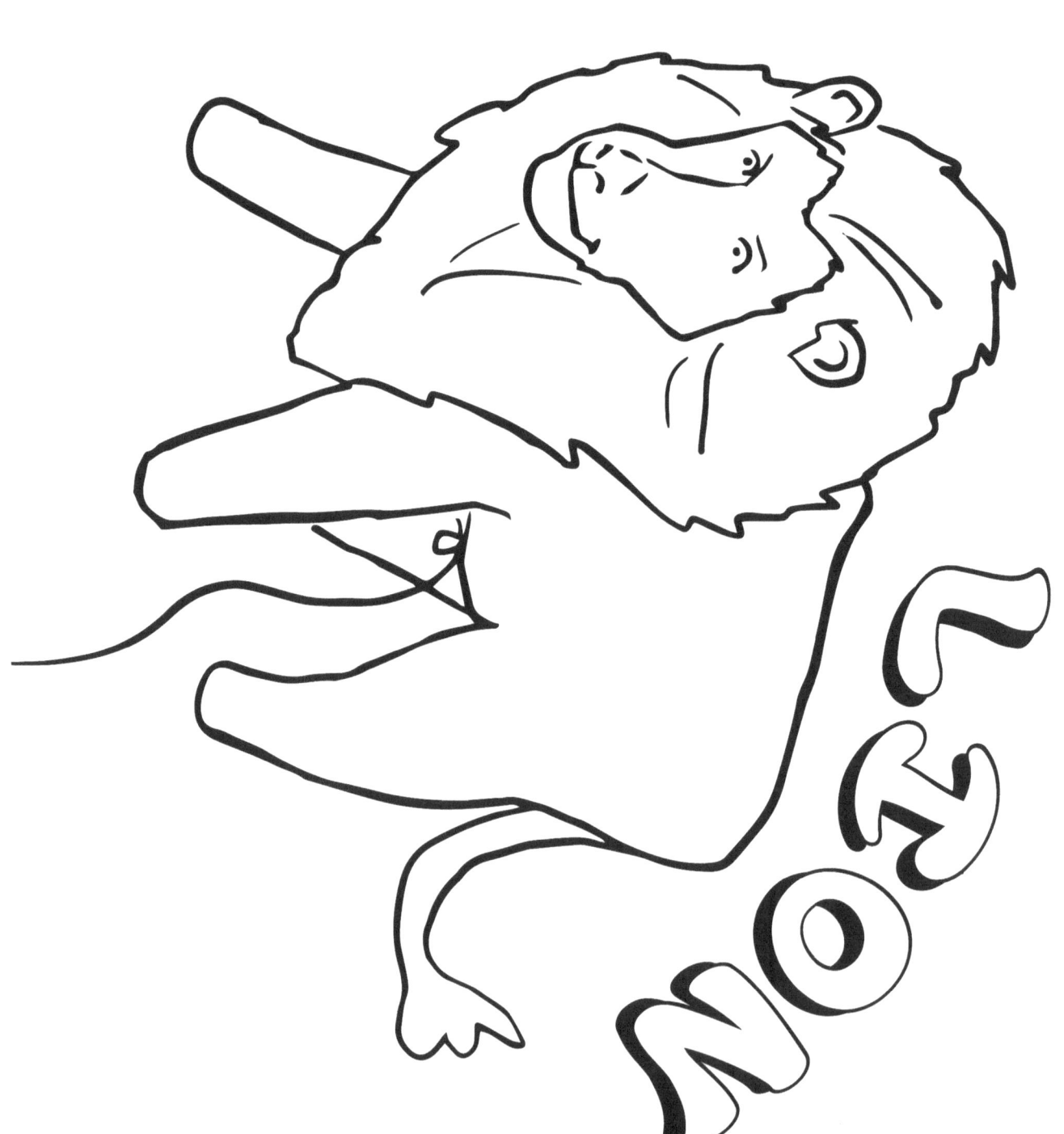

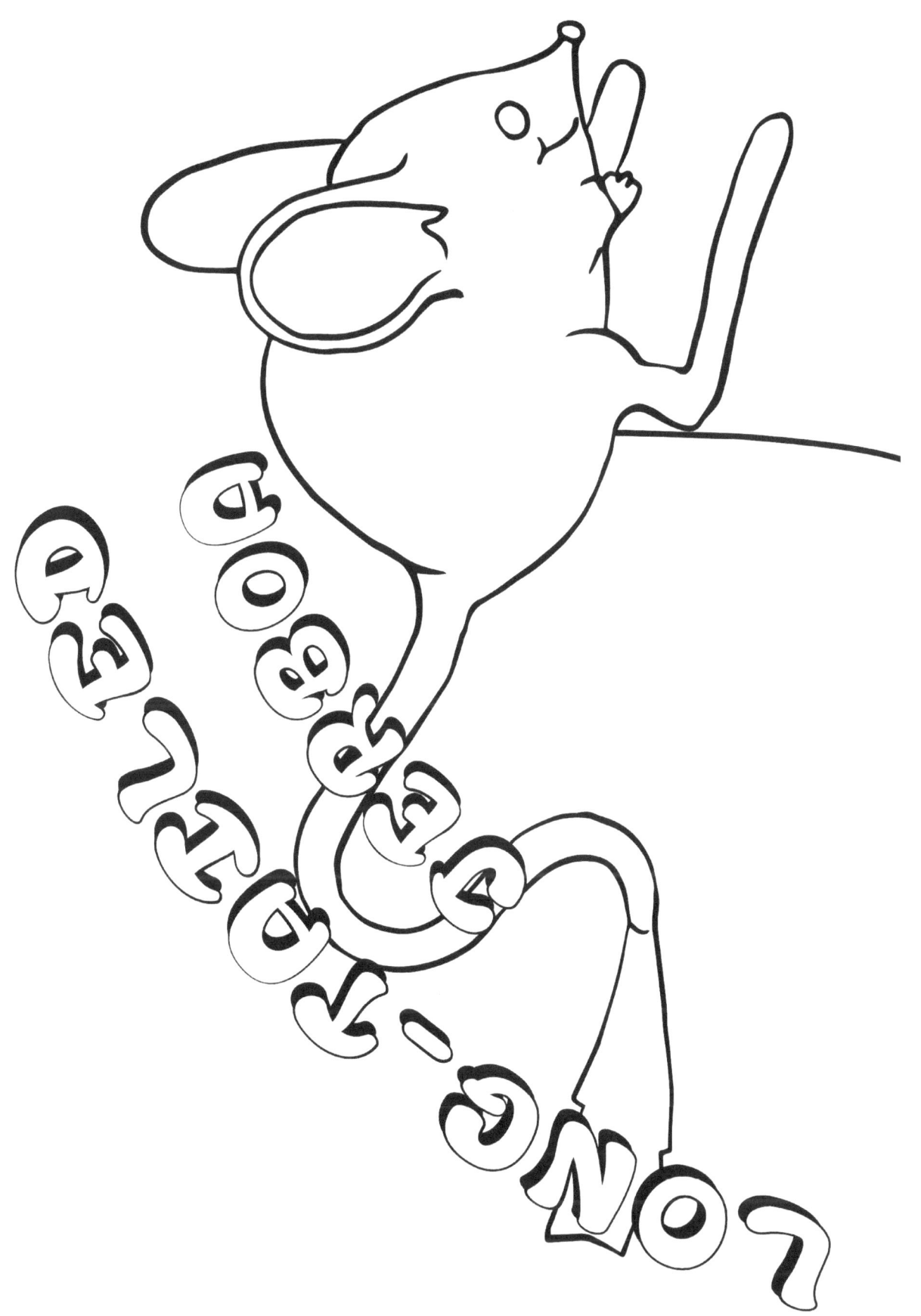

LONG-EARED BOG

MOUNTAIN GOAT

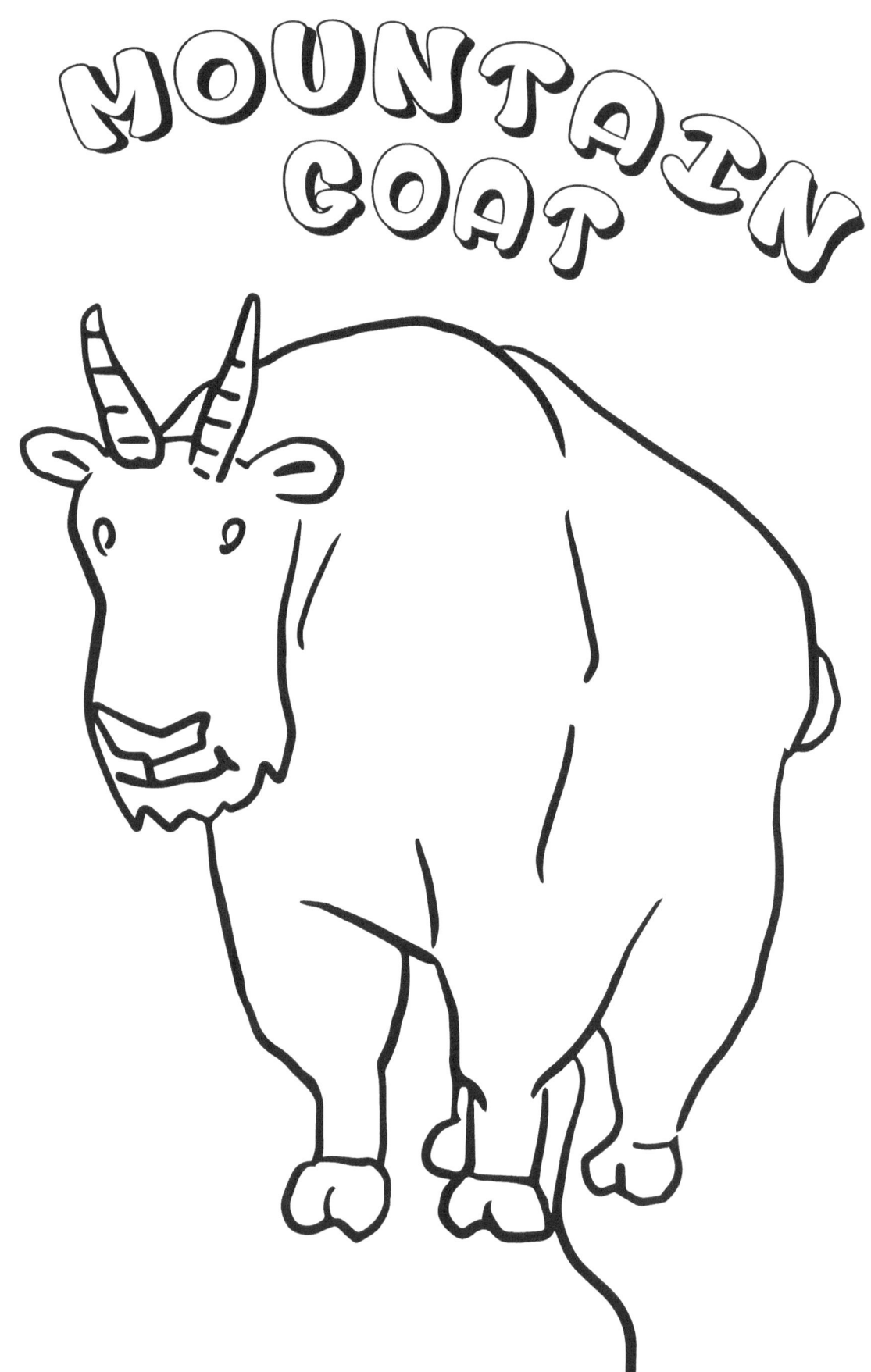

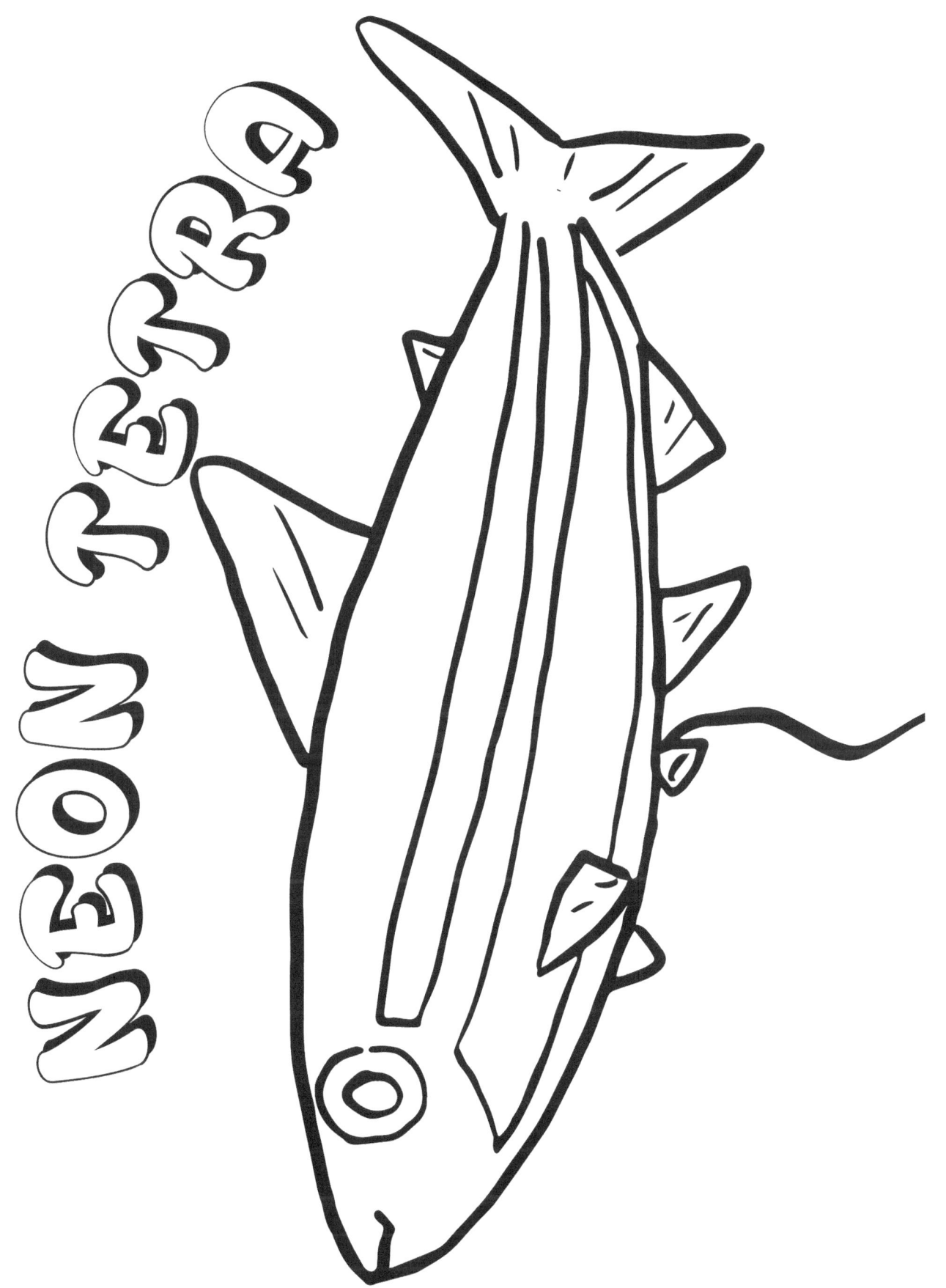

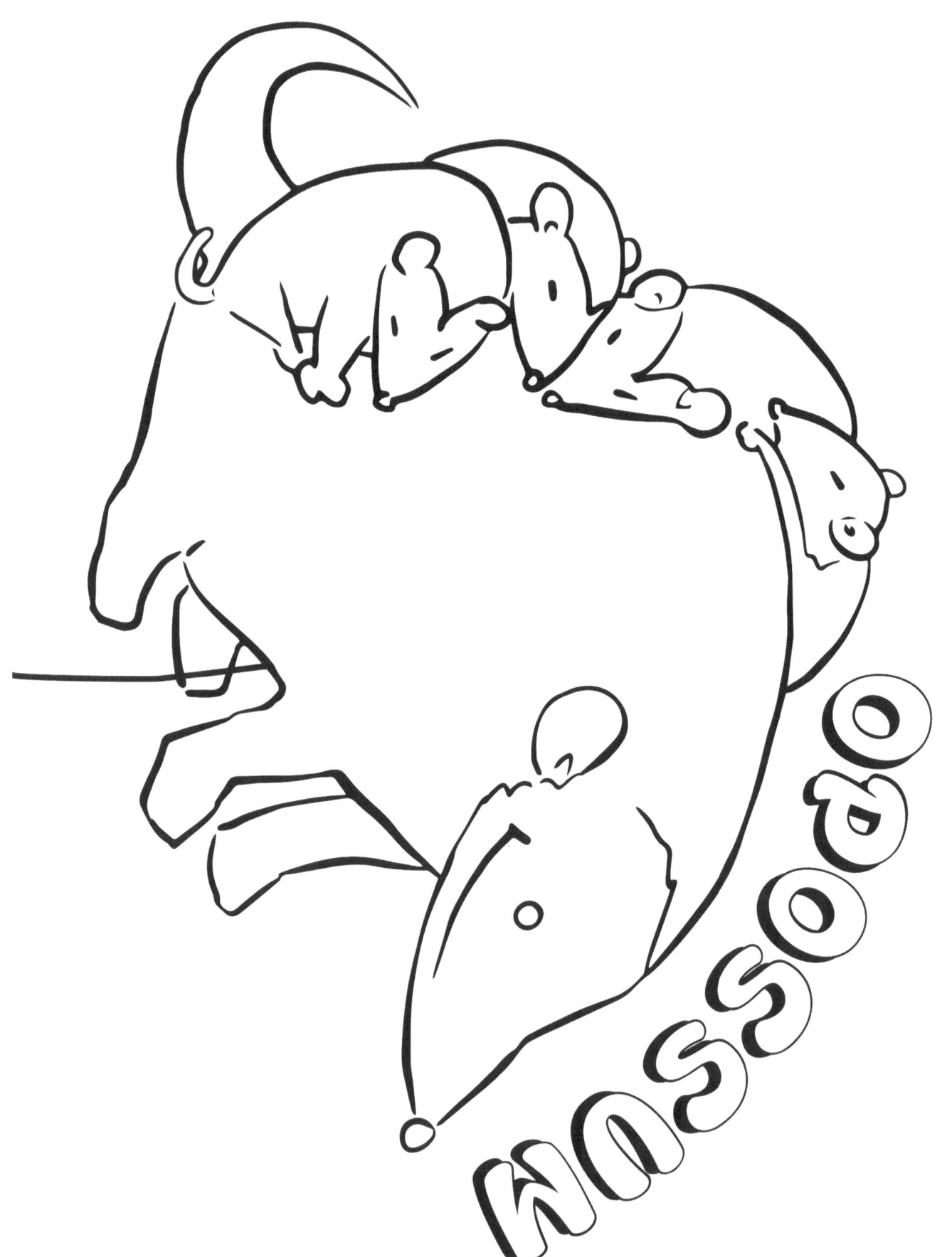

OPOSSUM

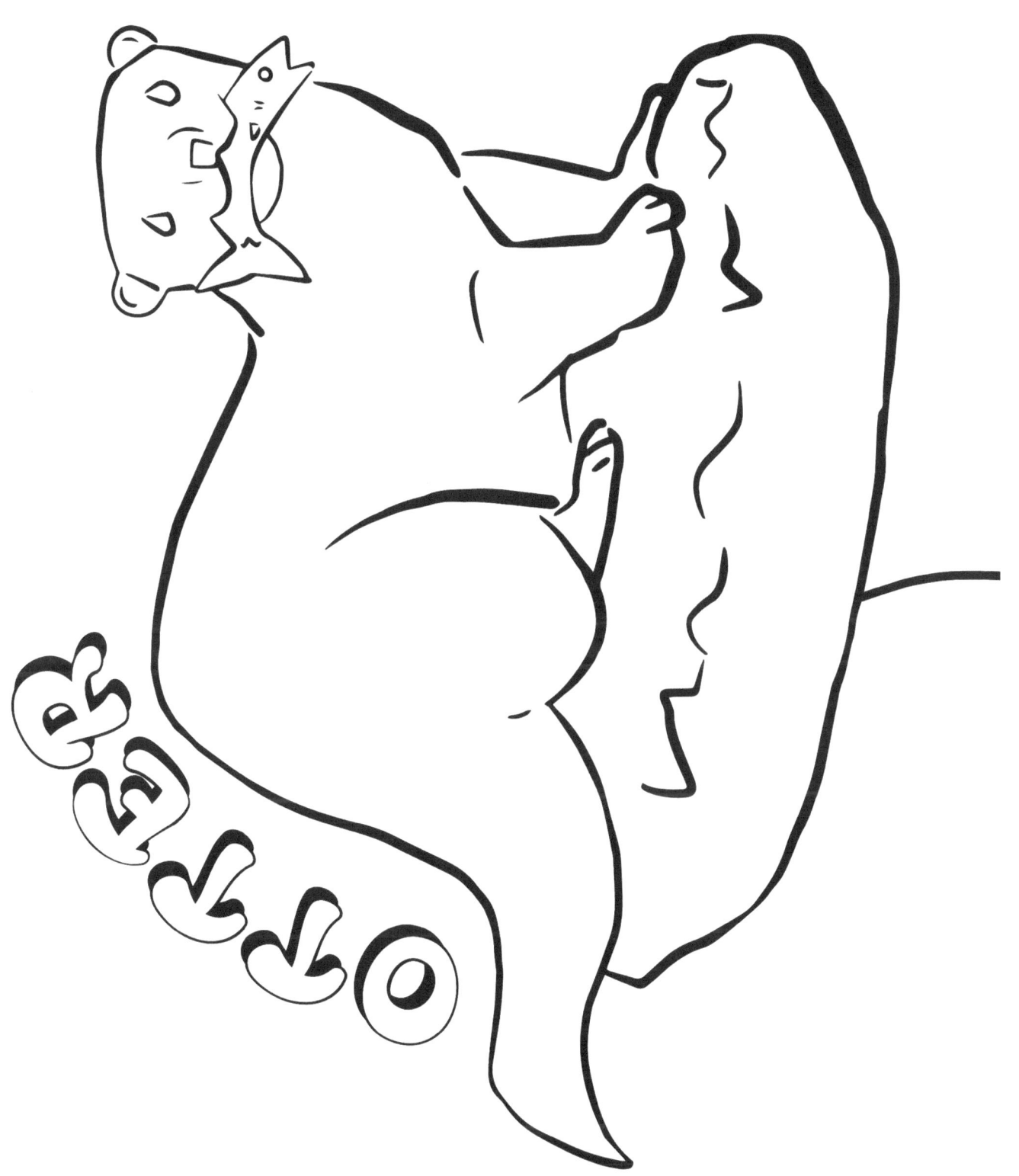

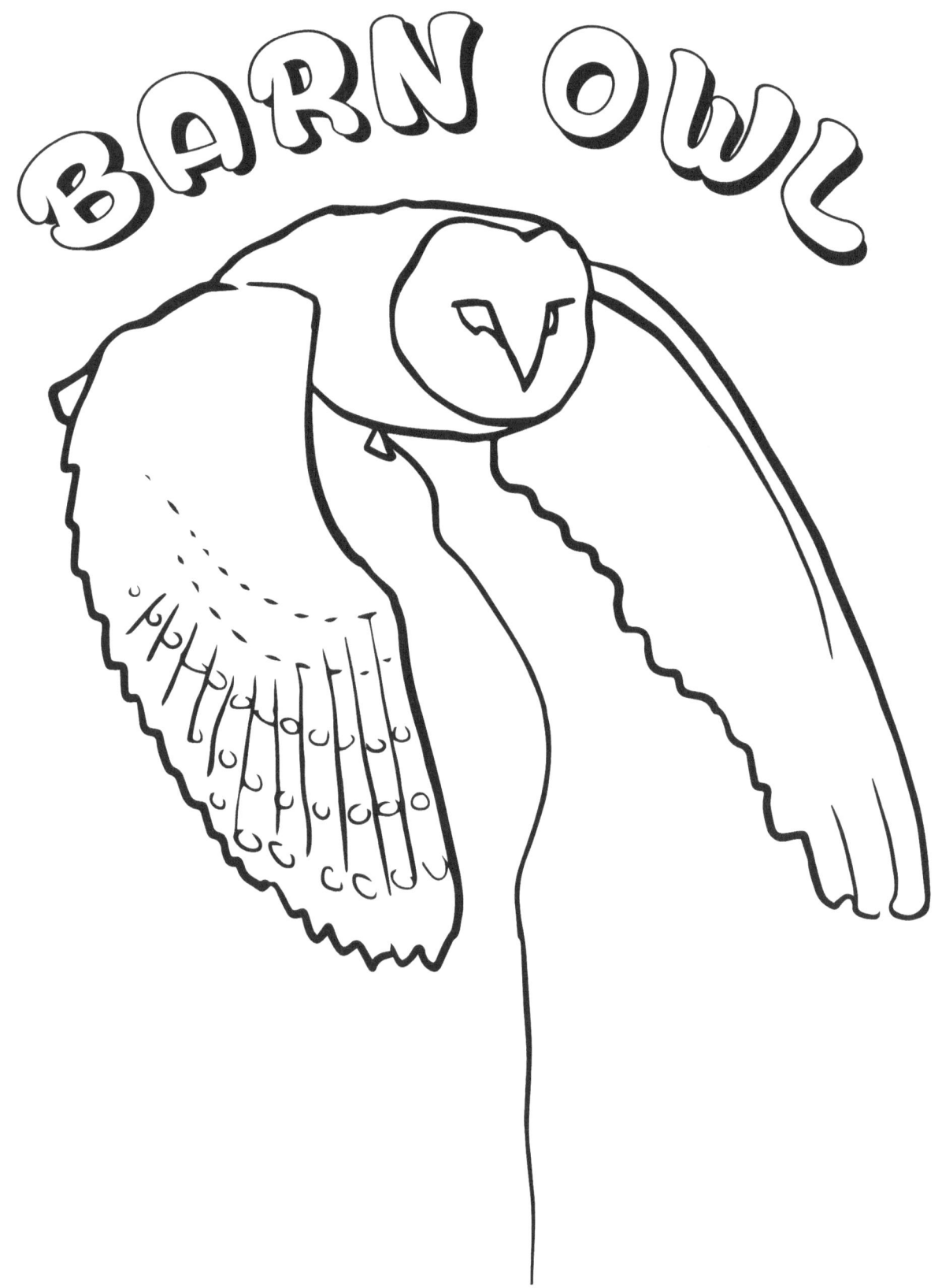

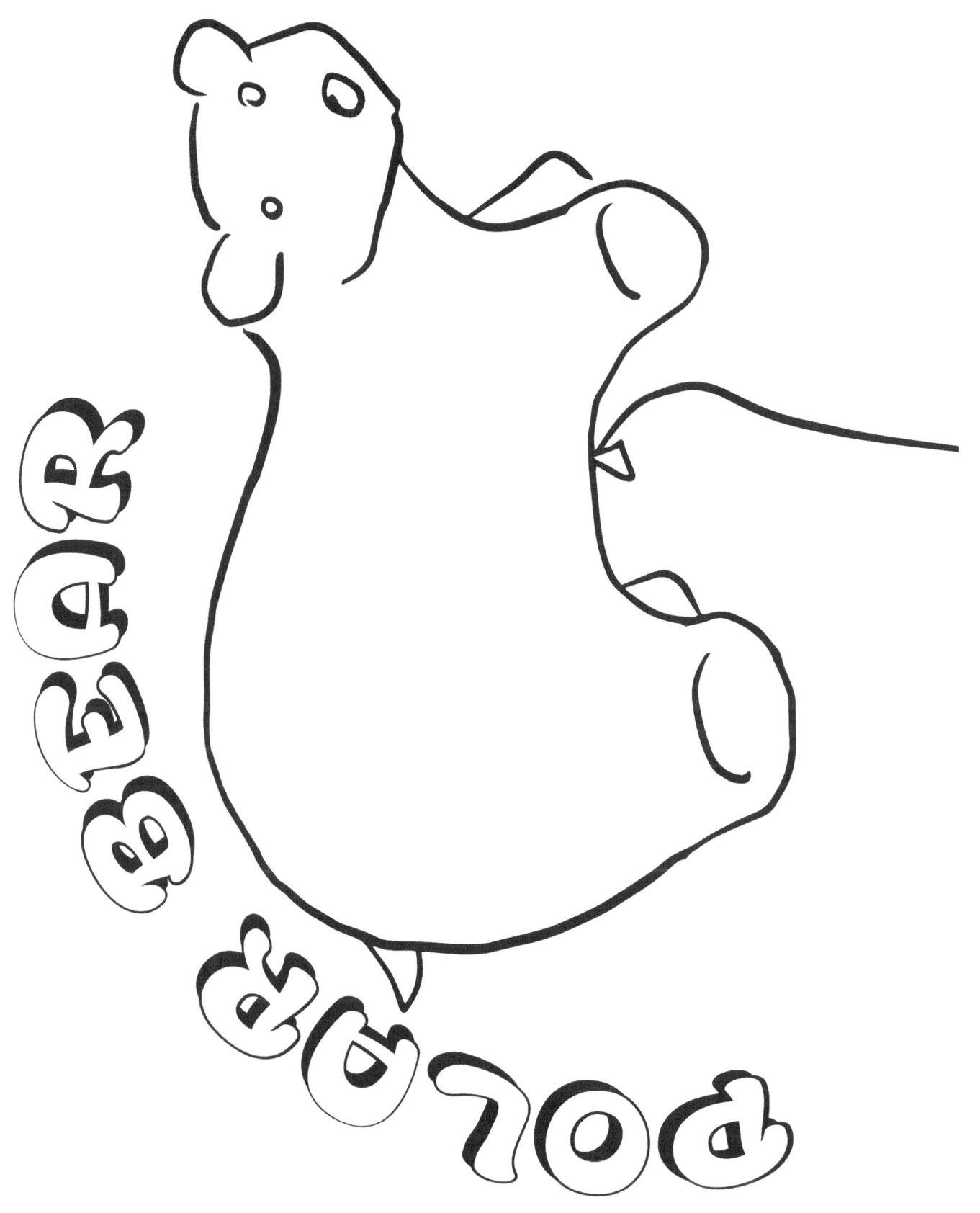

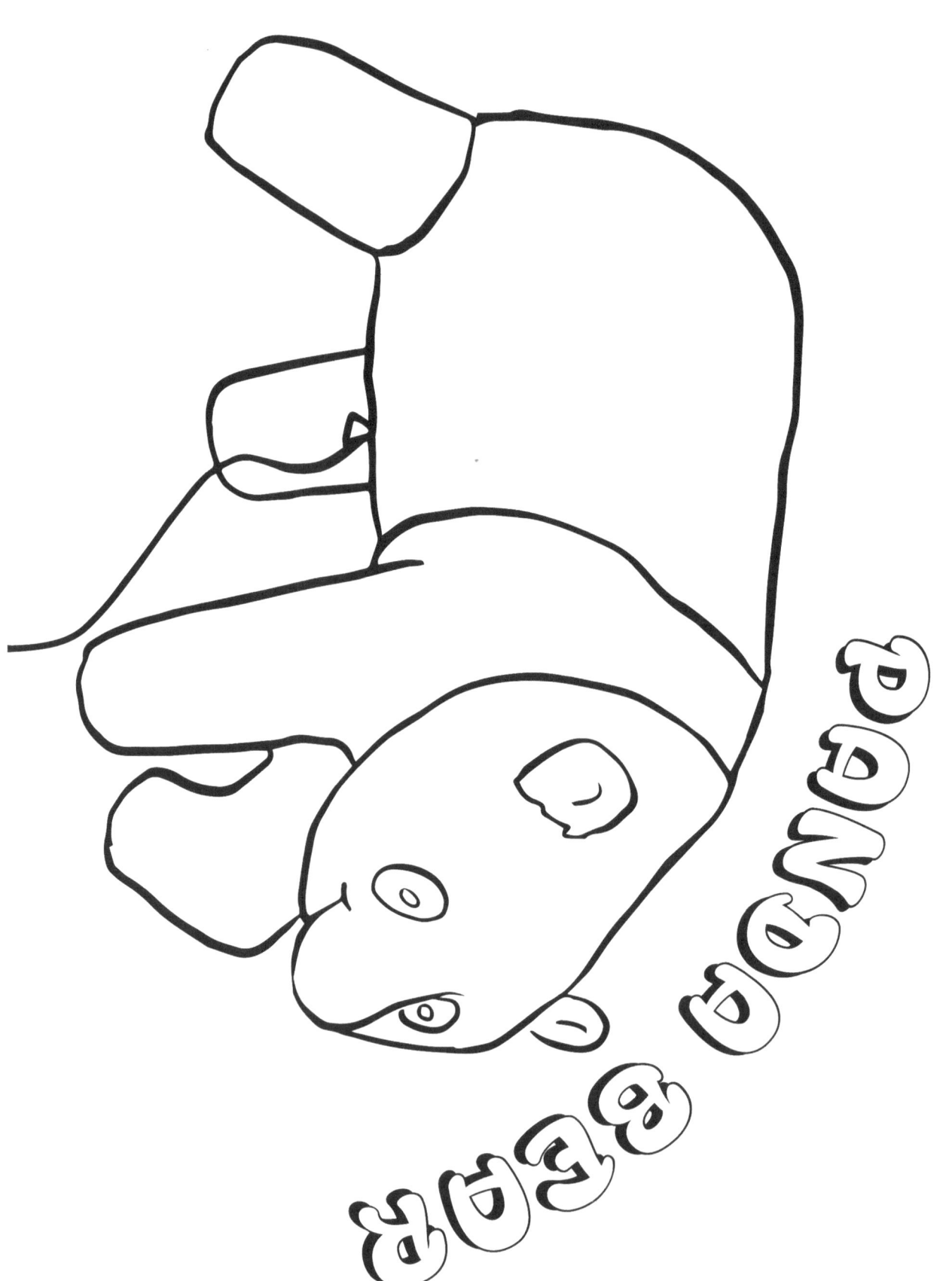

PANDA BEAR

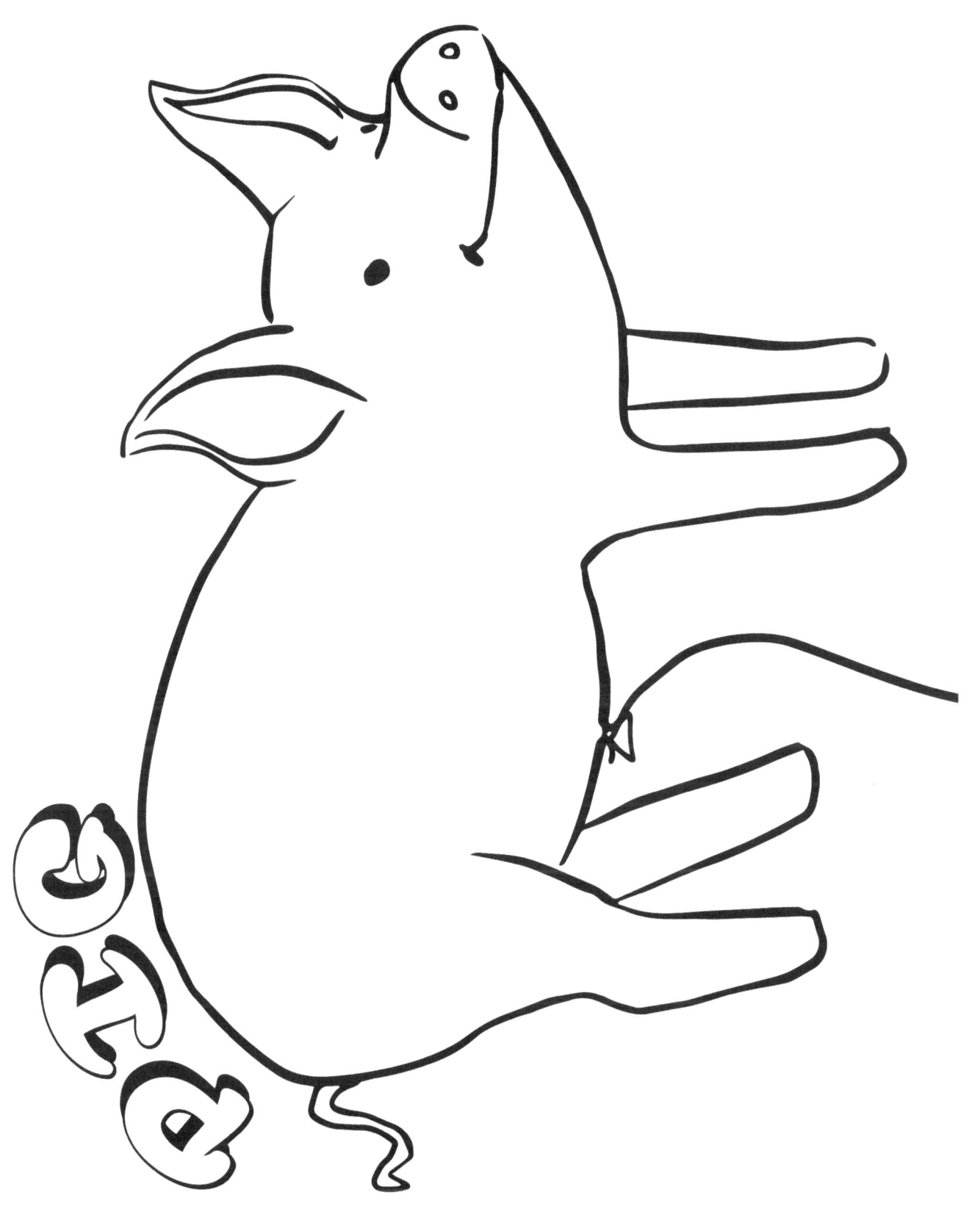

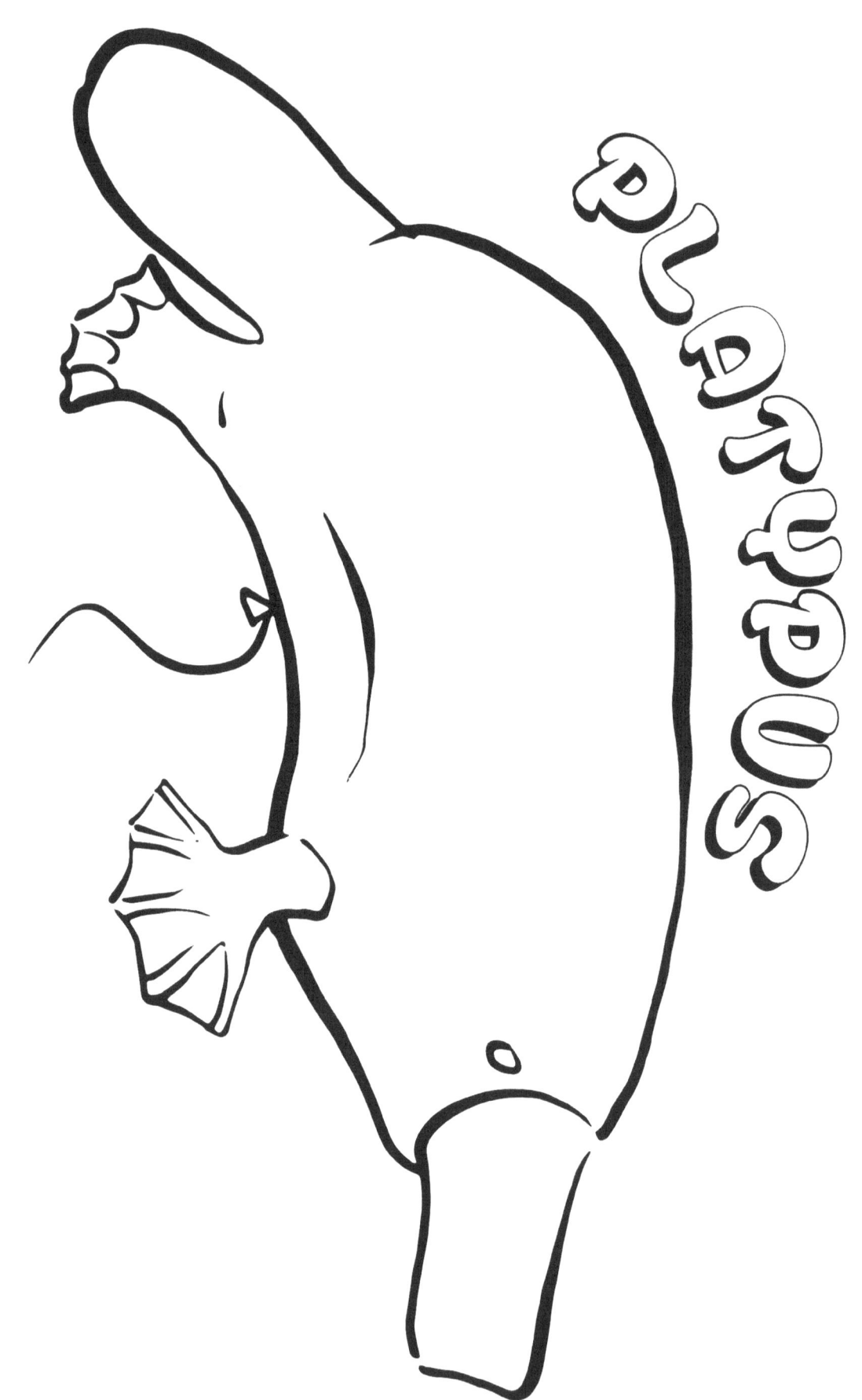

PLATYPUS

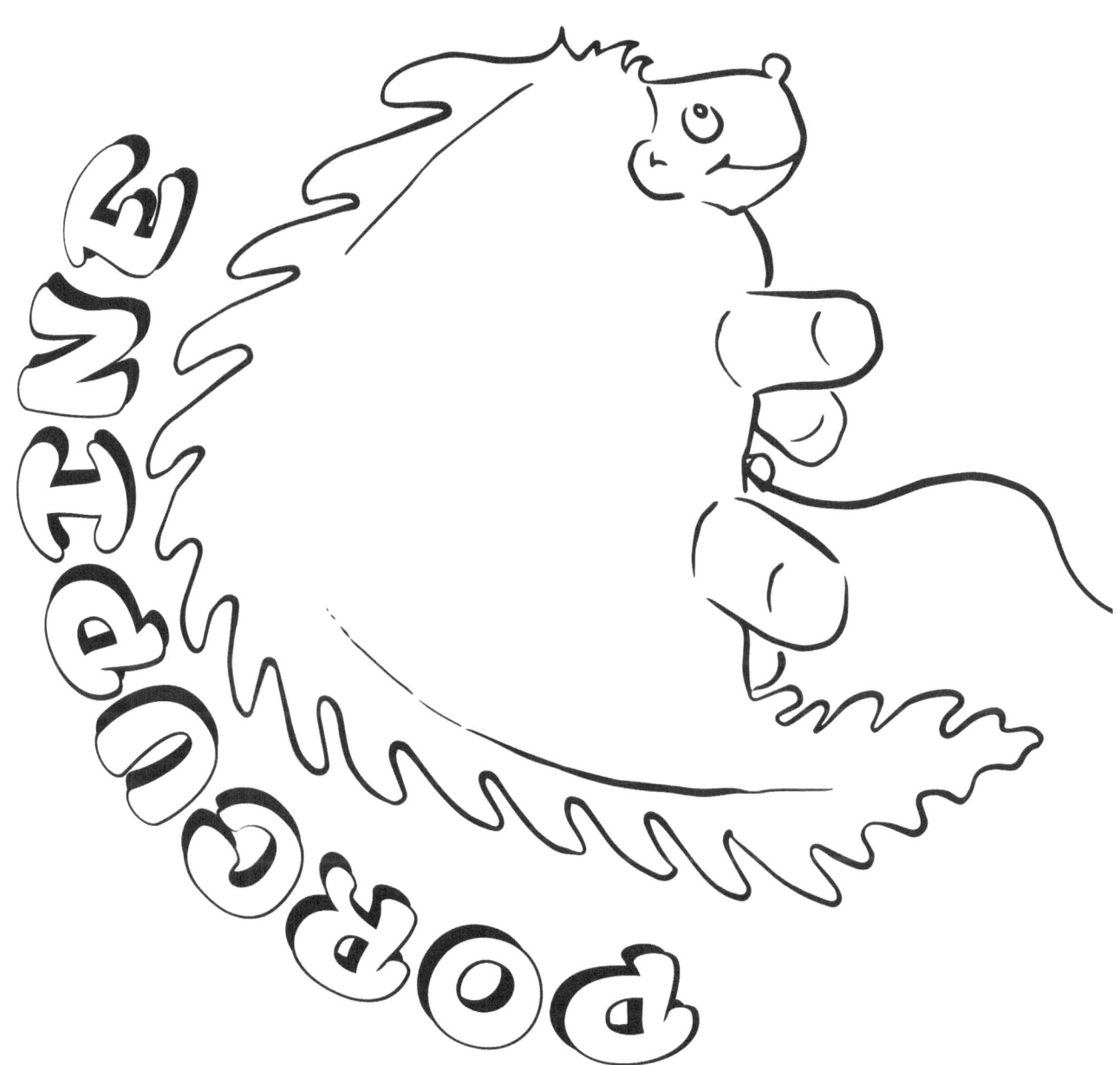

PORCUPINE

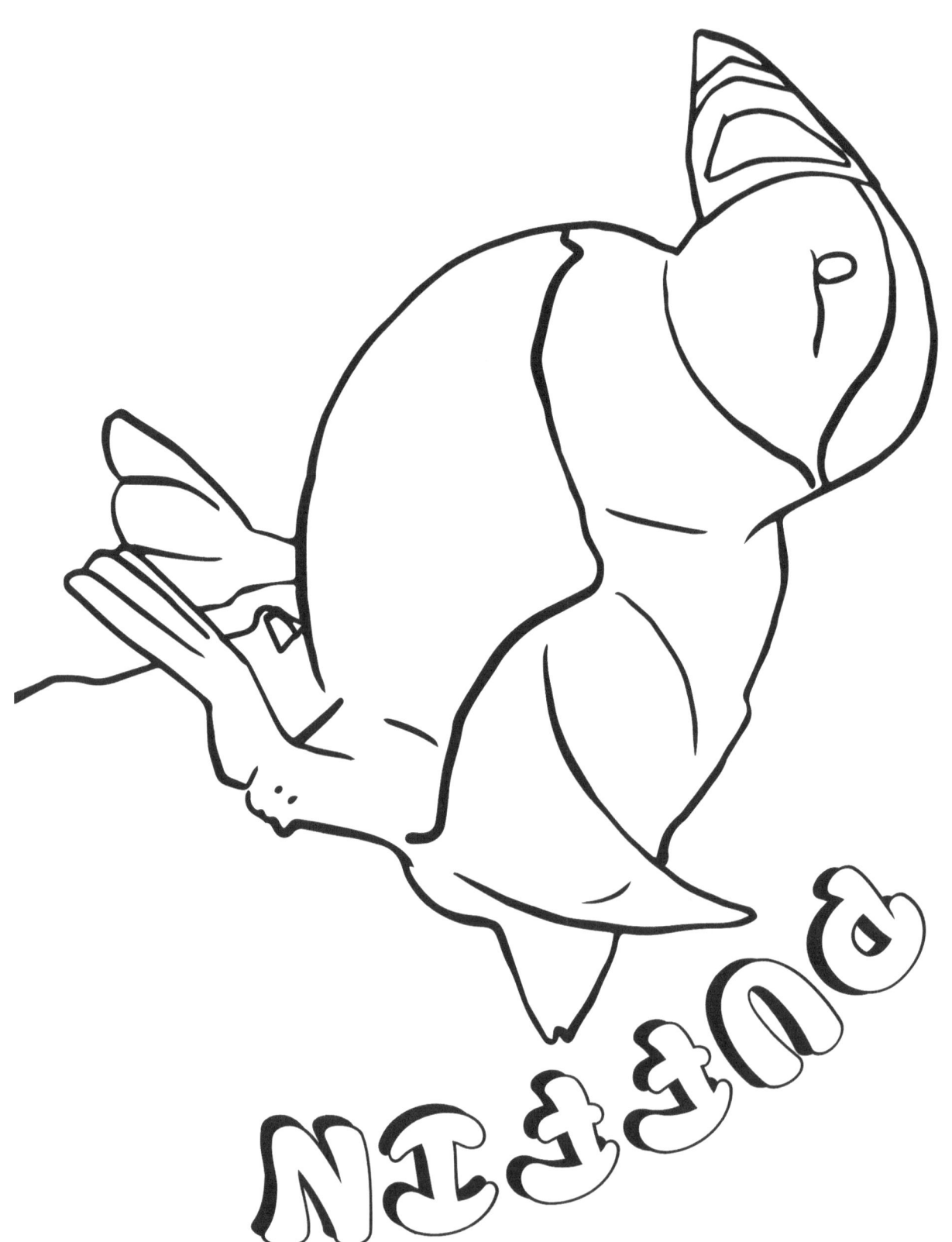

PUFFIN

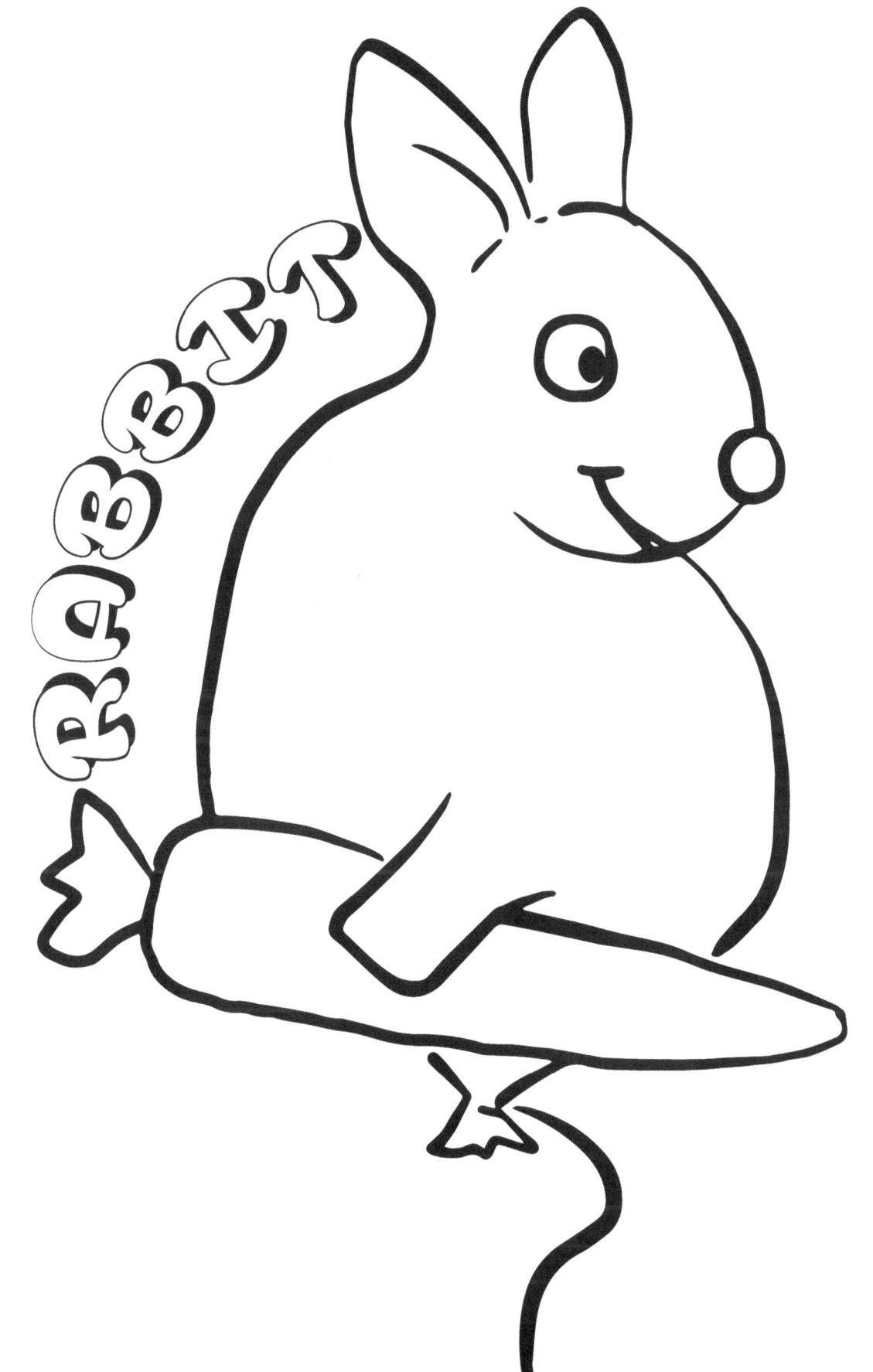

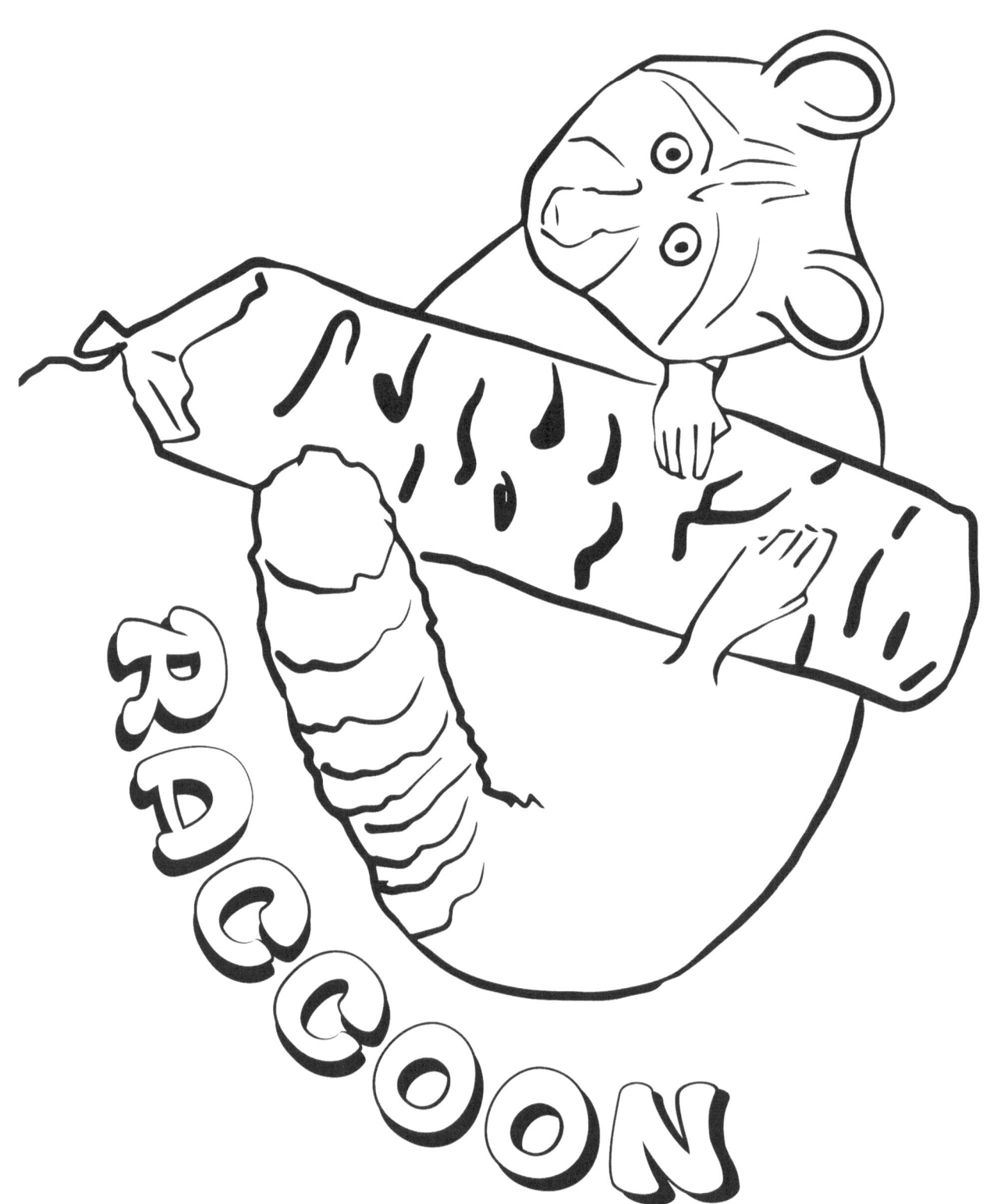

RACCOON

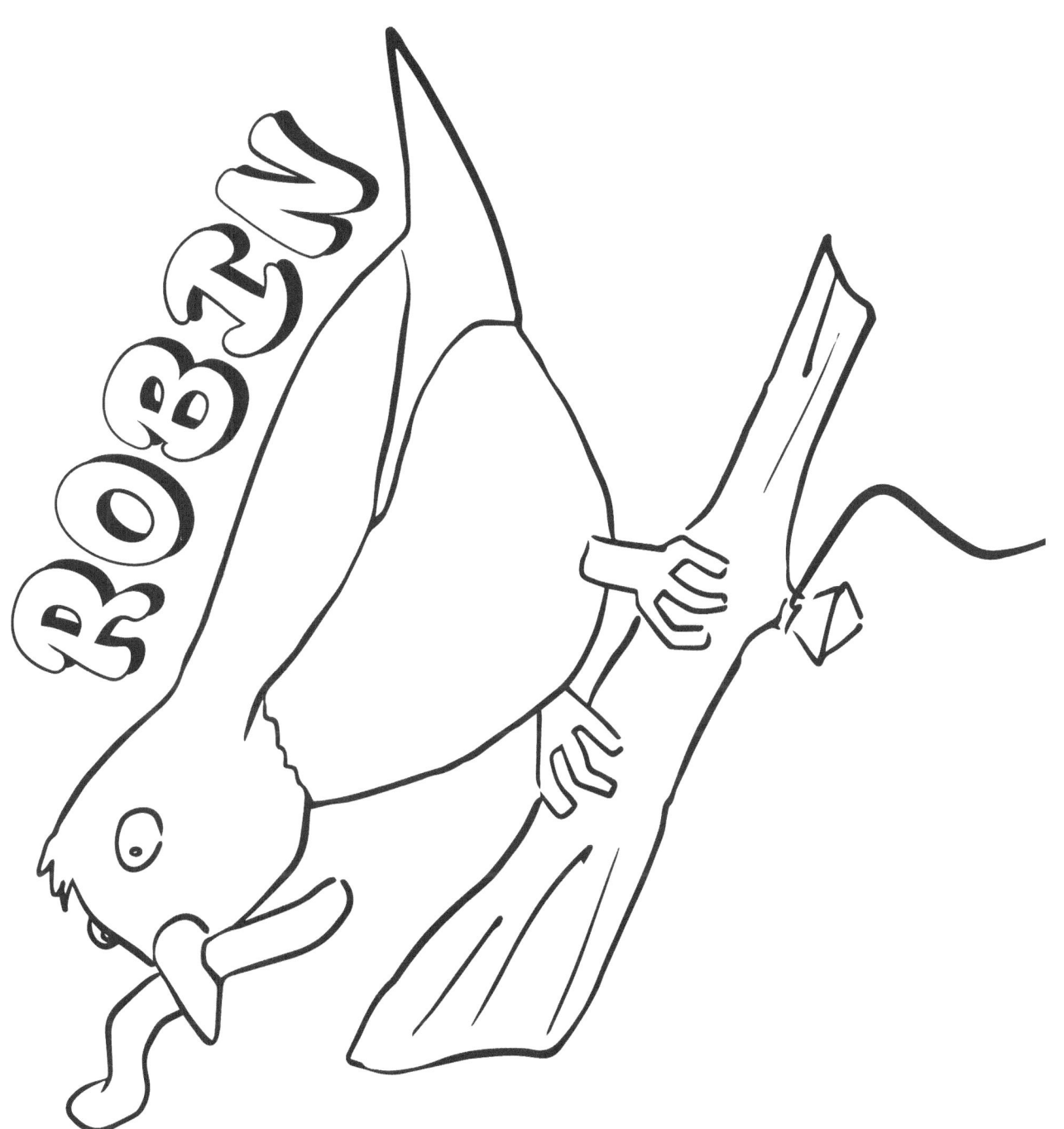

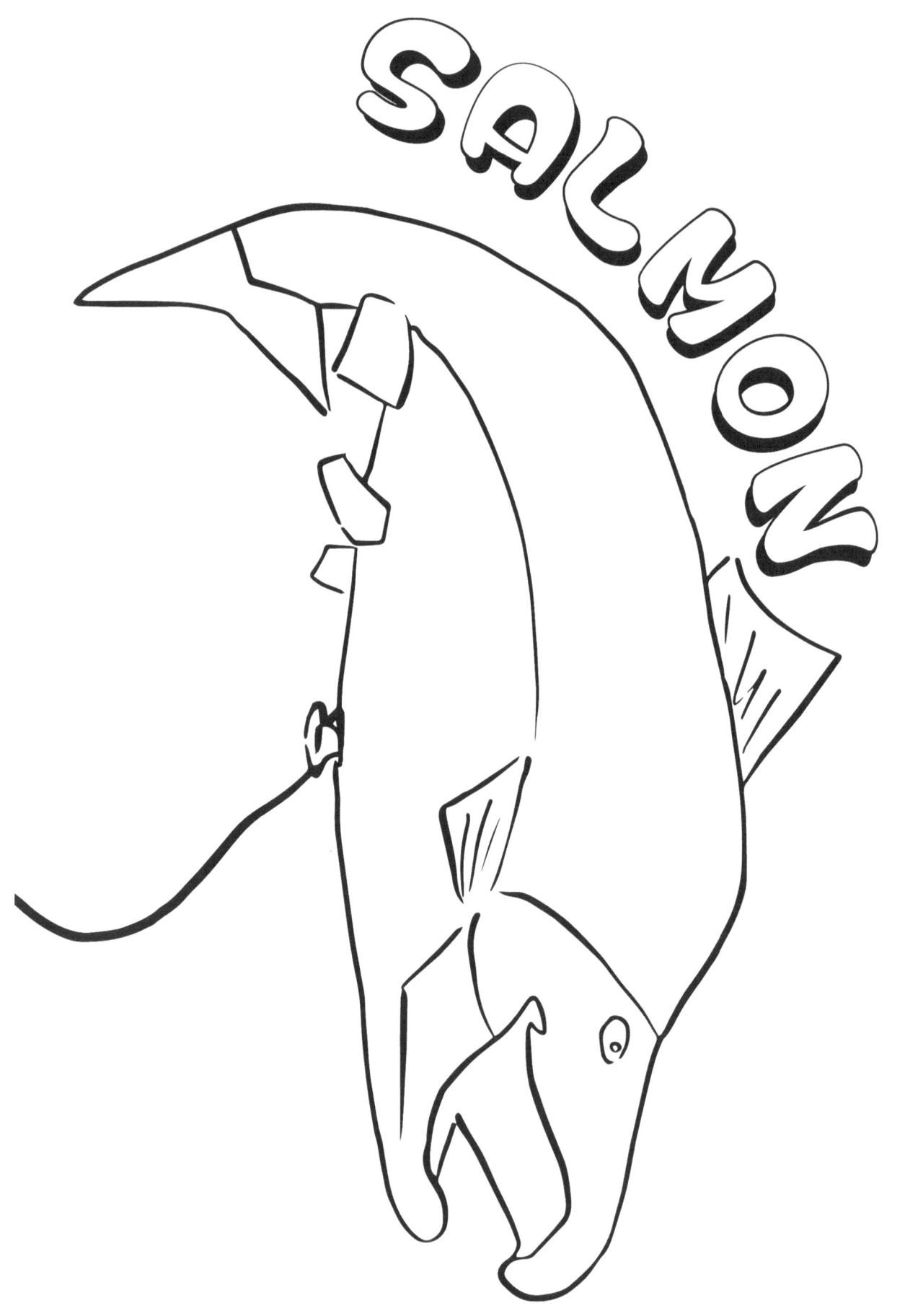

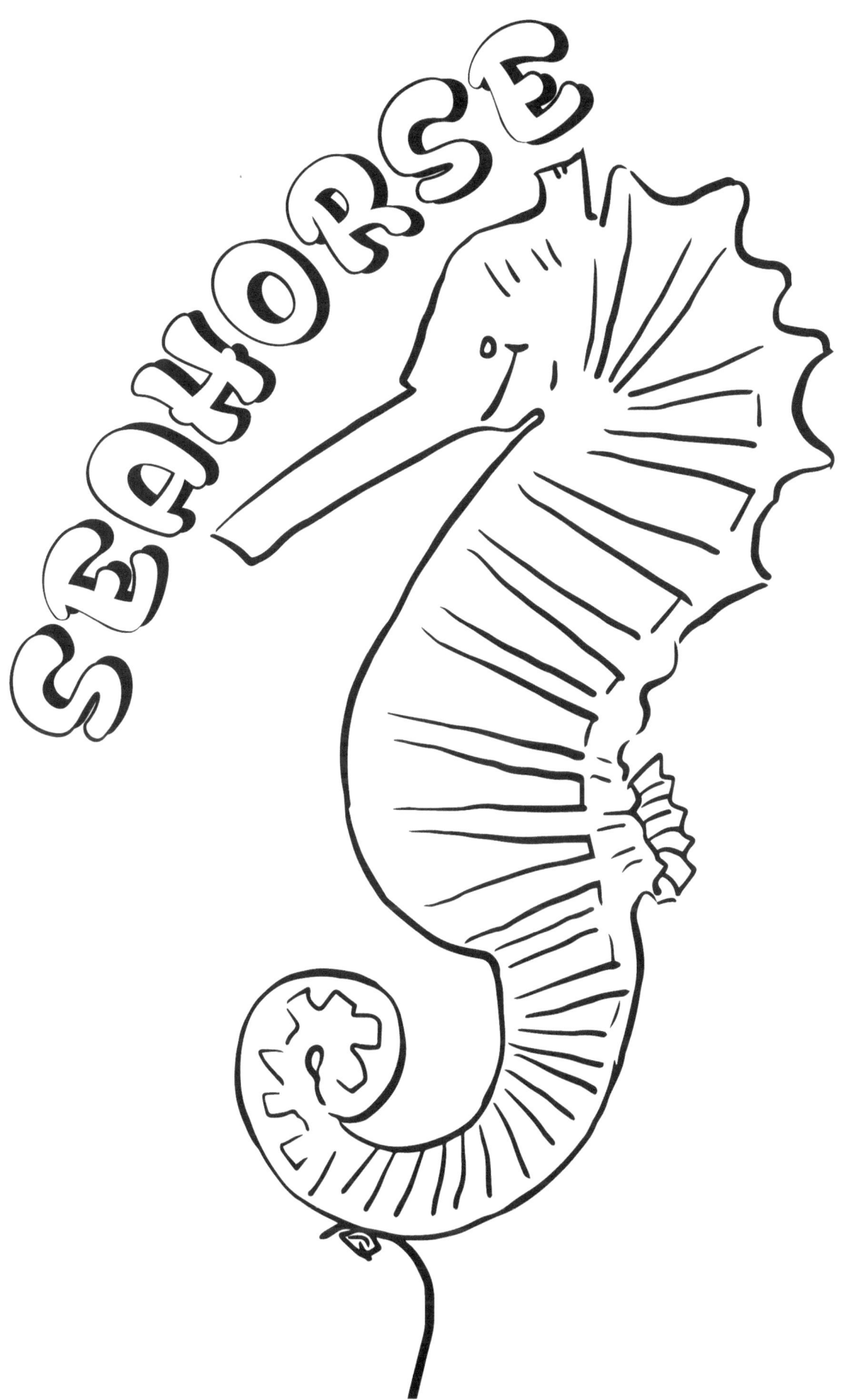

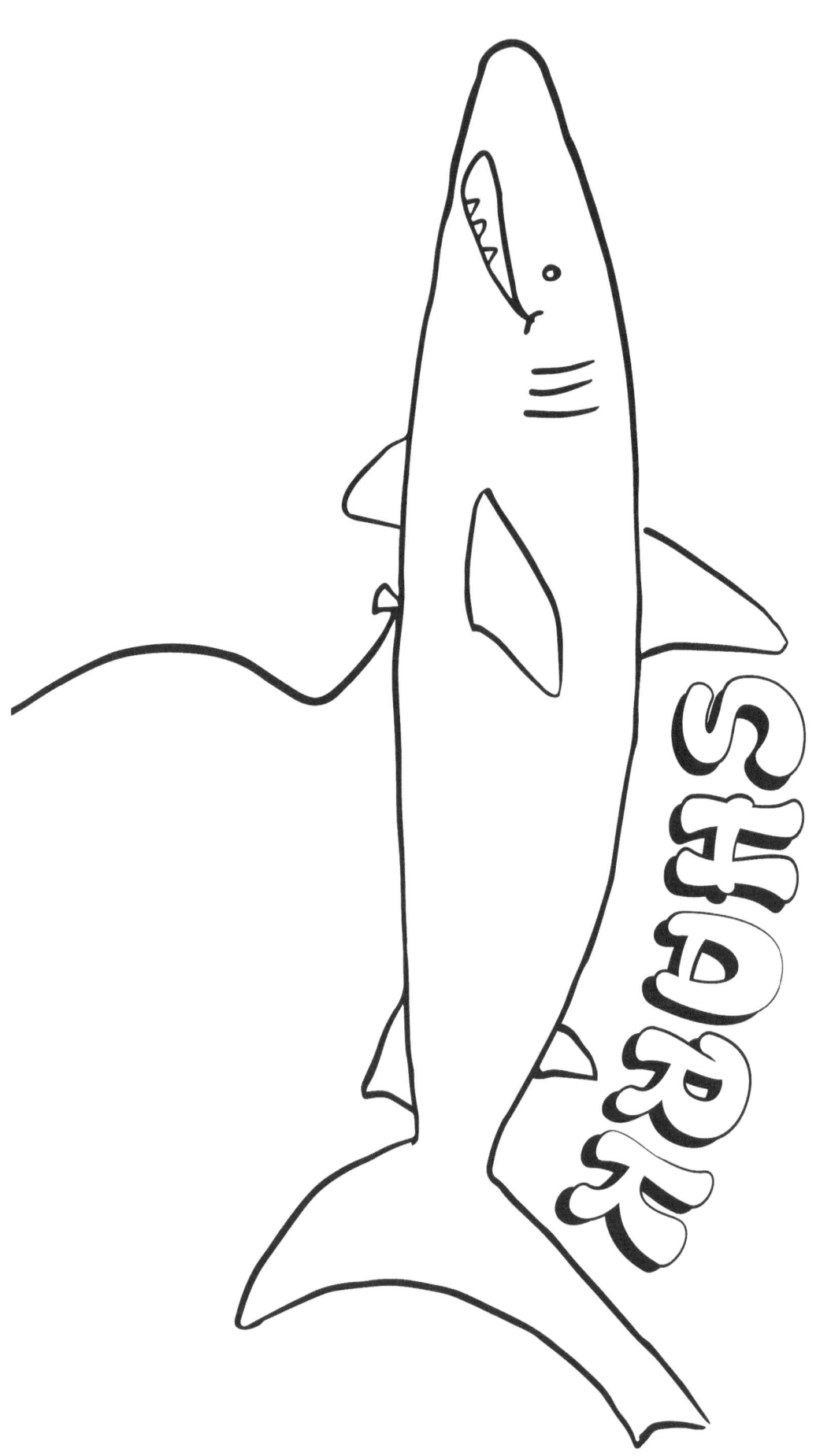

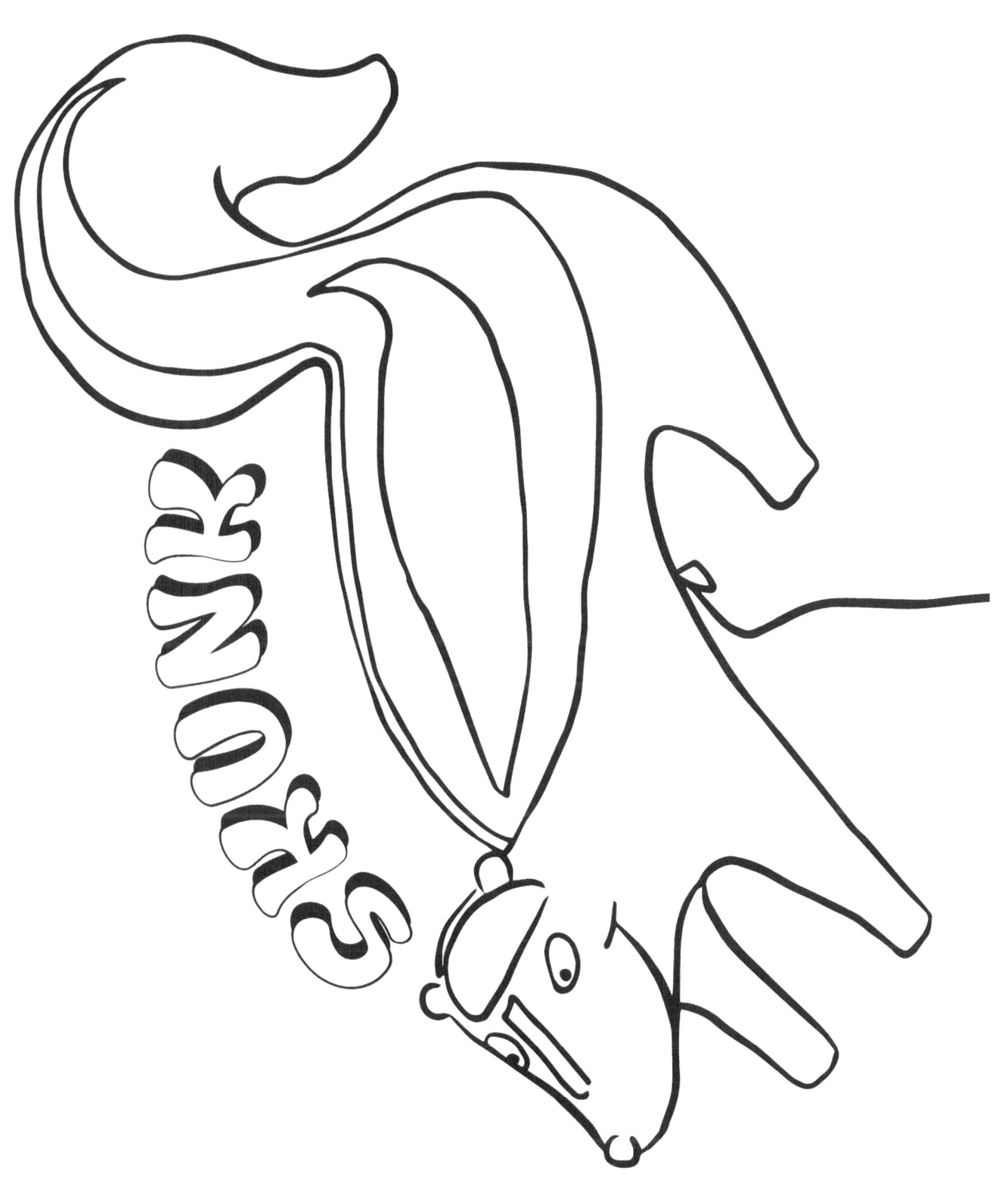

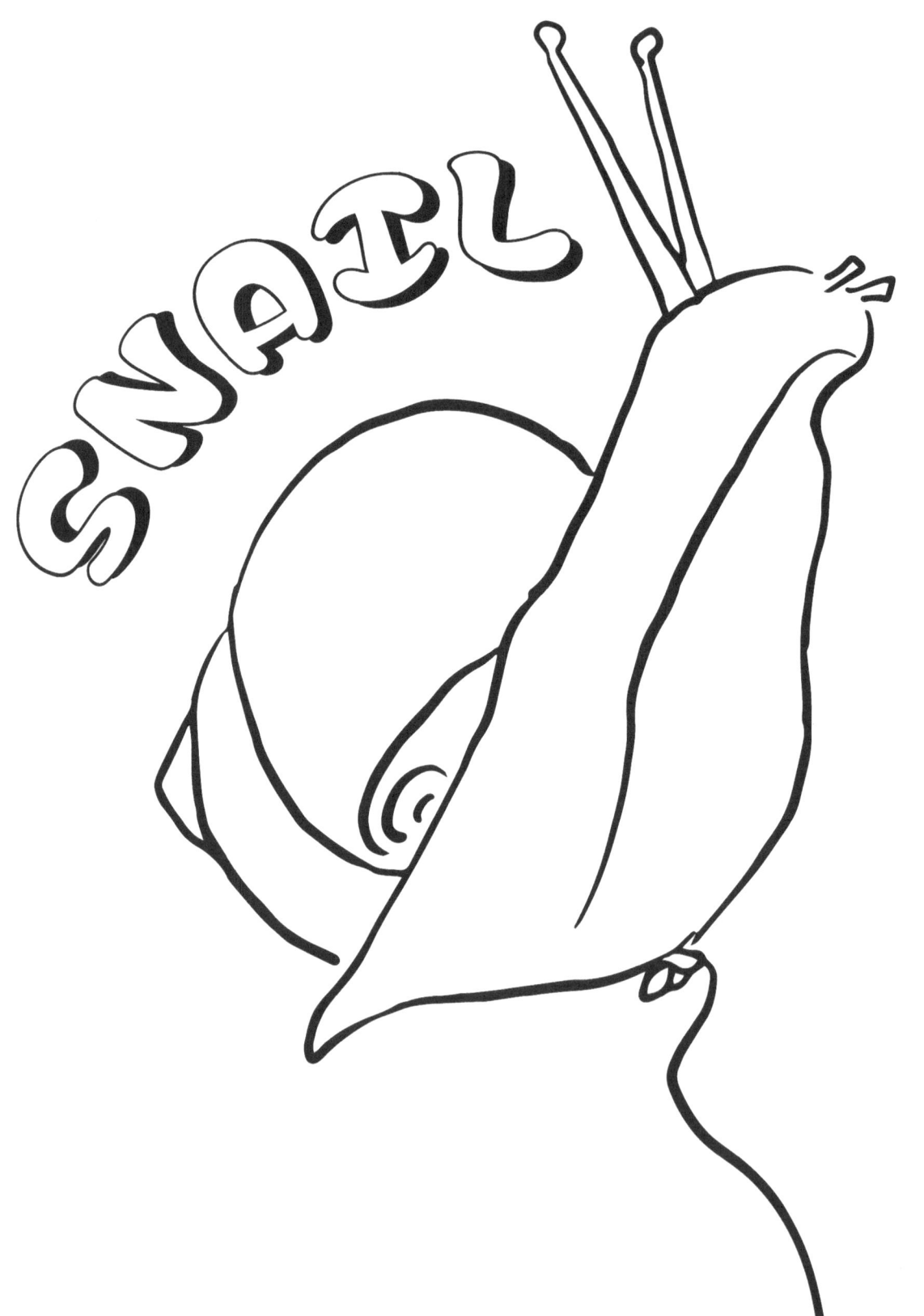

SQUIRREL

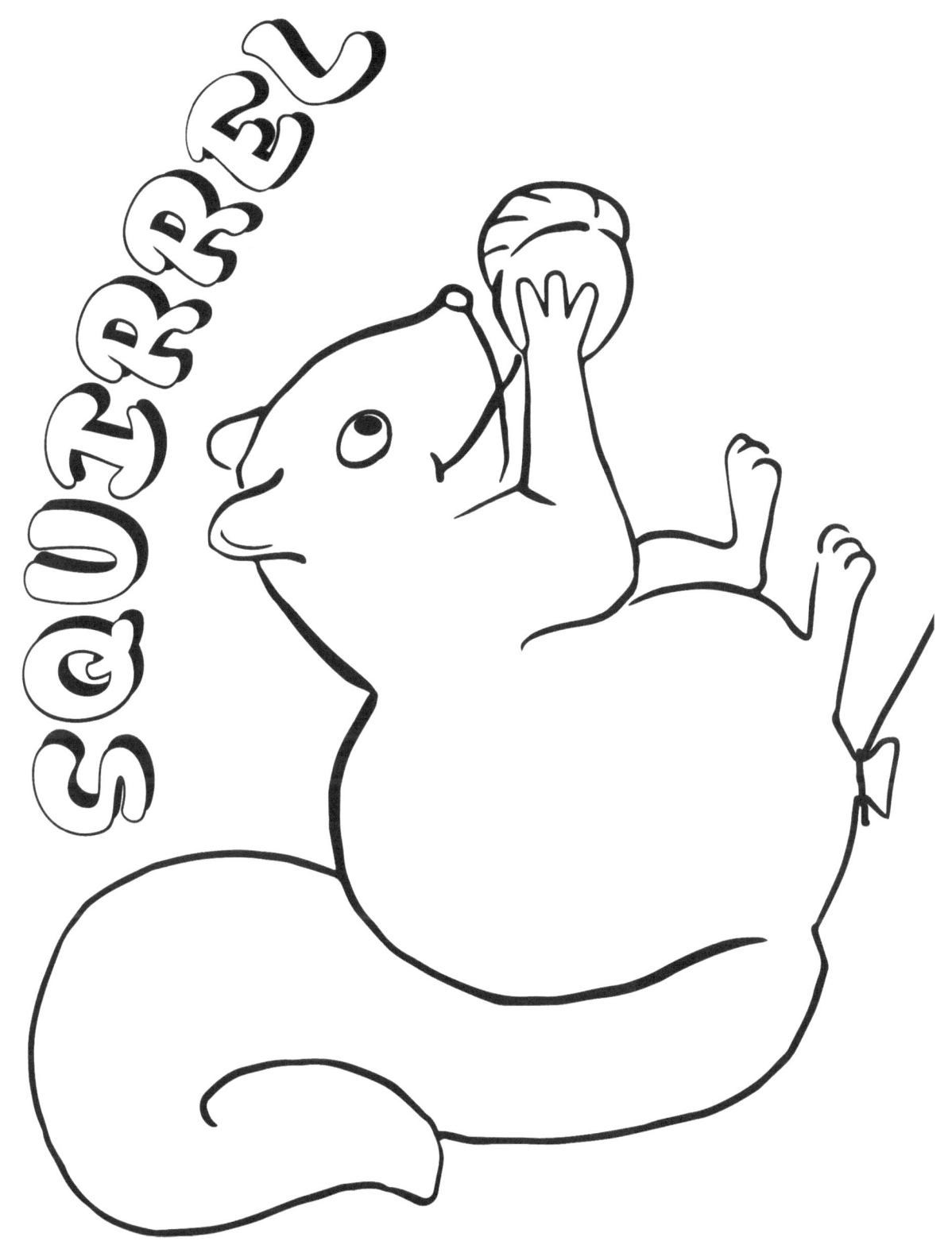

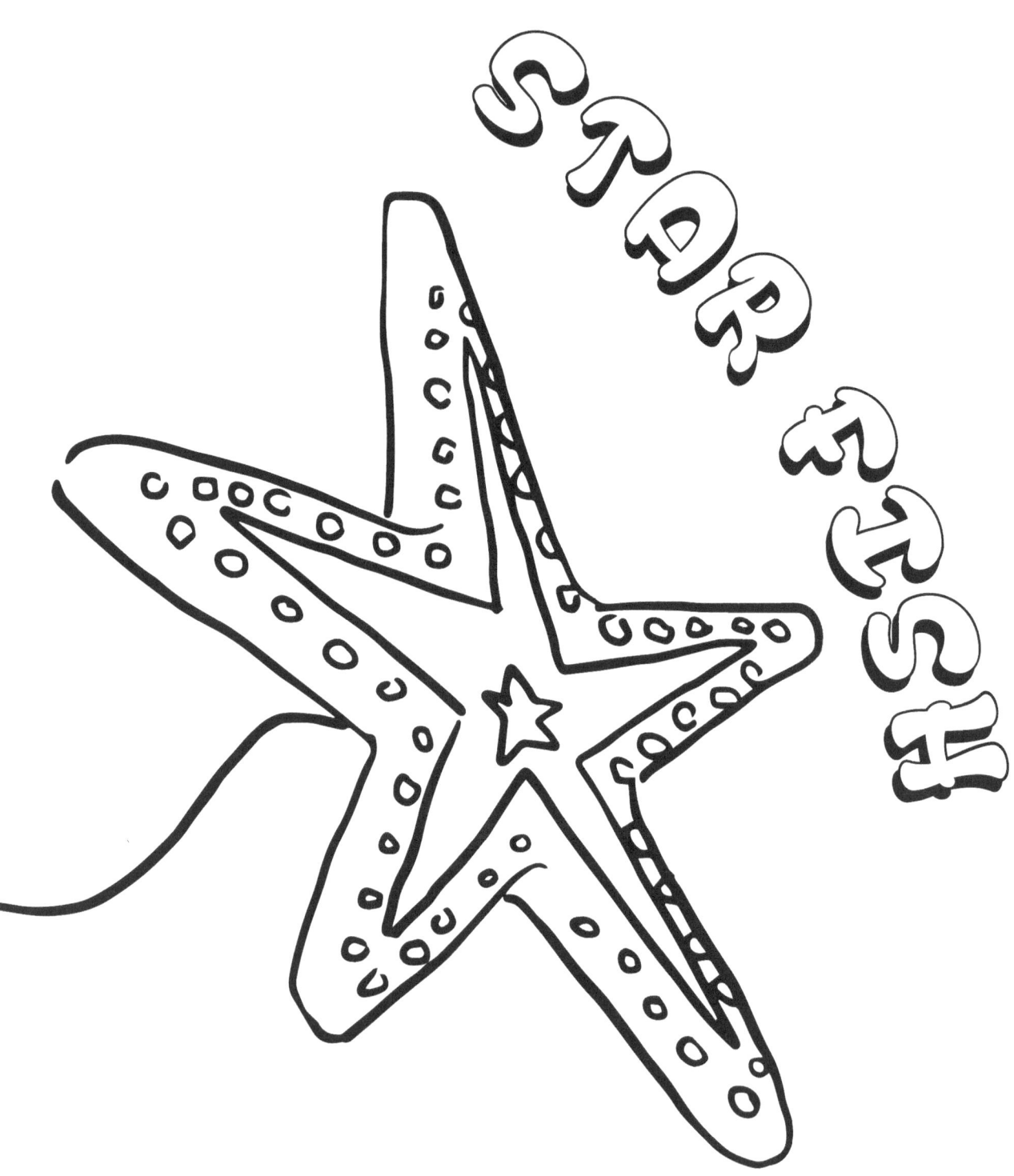

STAR FISH

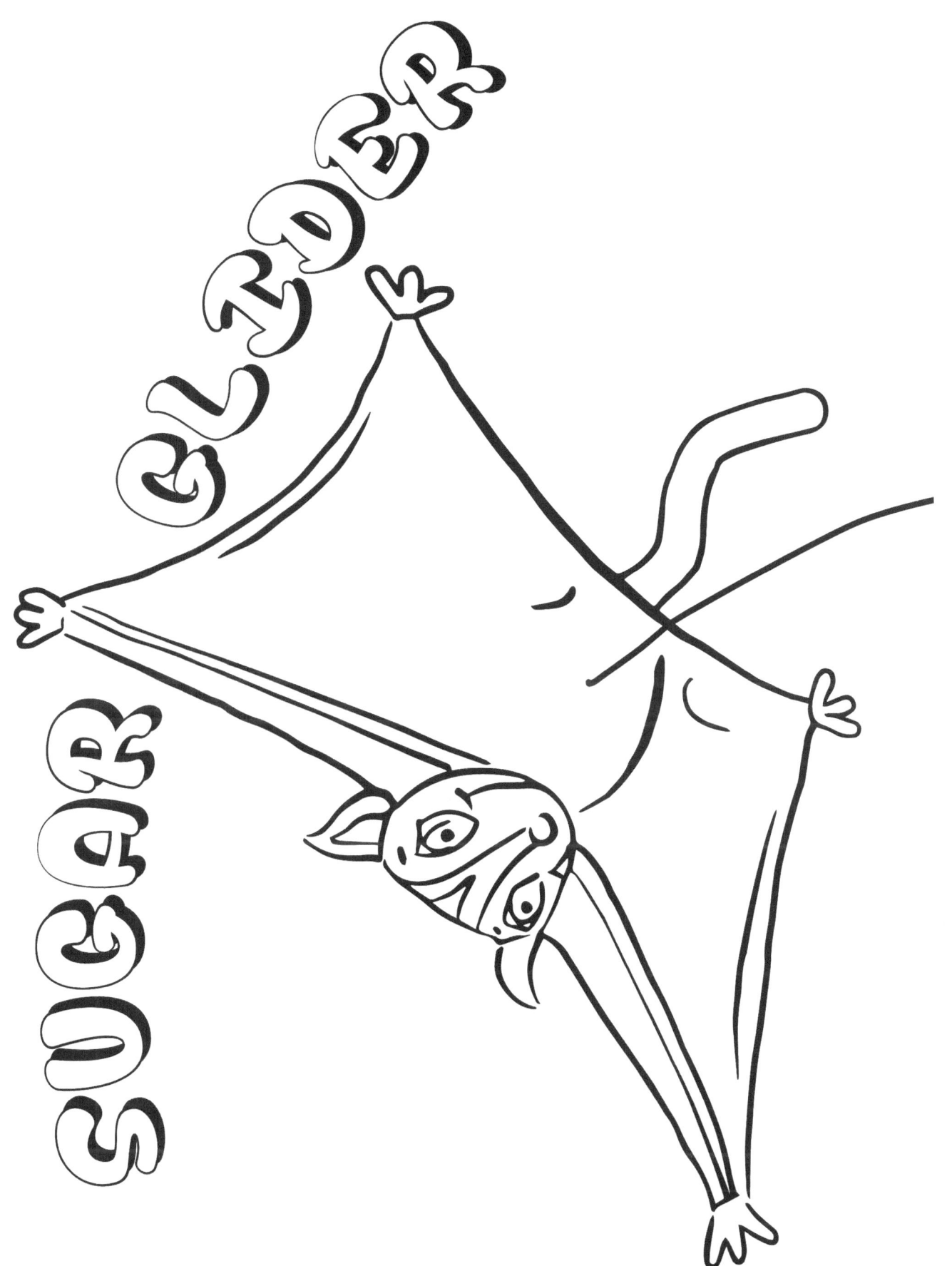

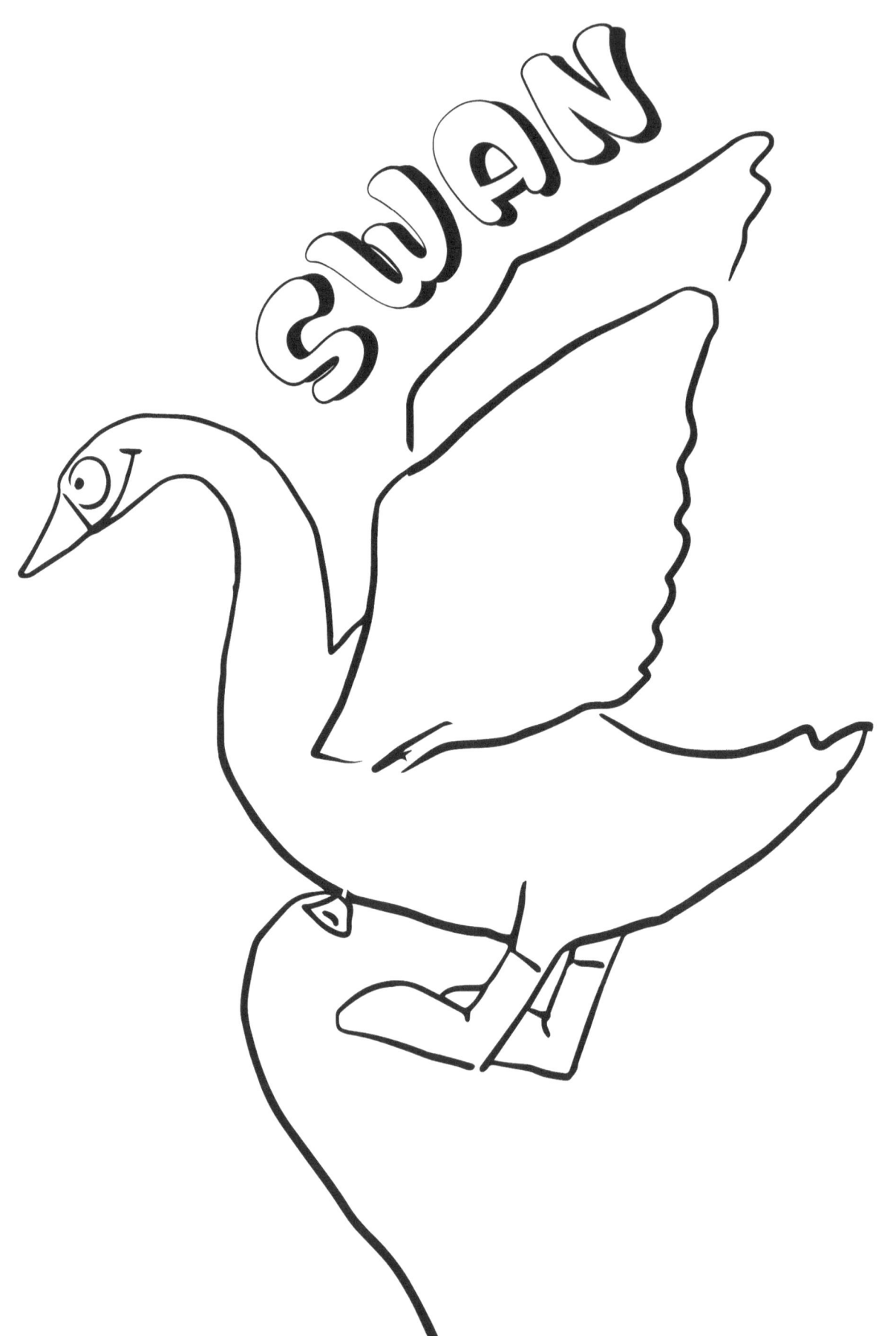

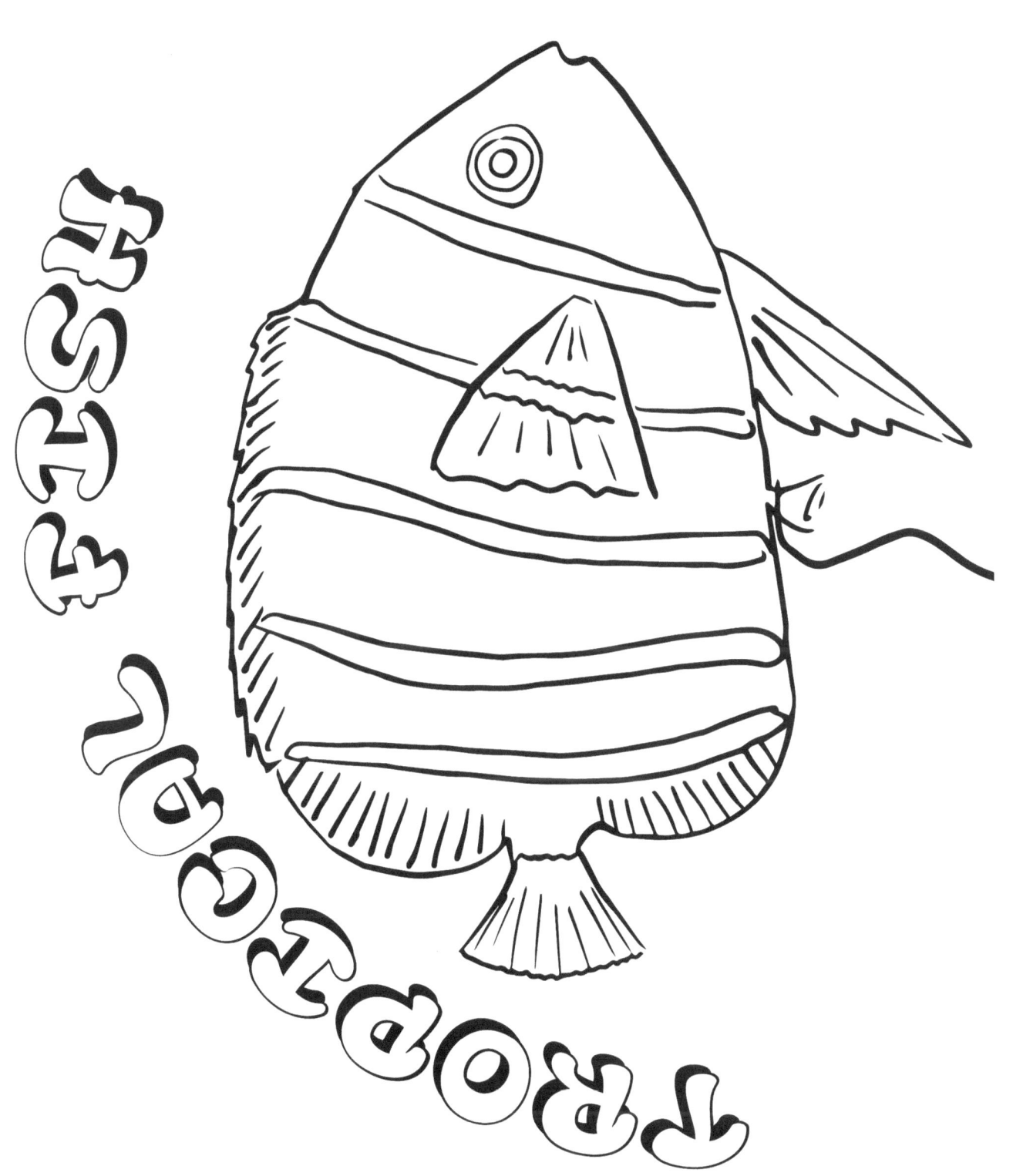

TROPICAL FISH

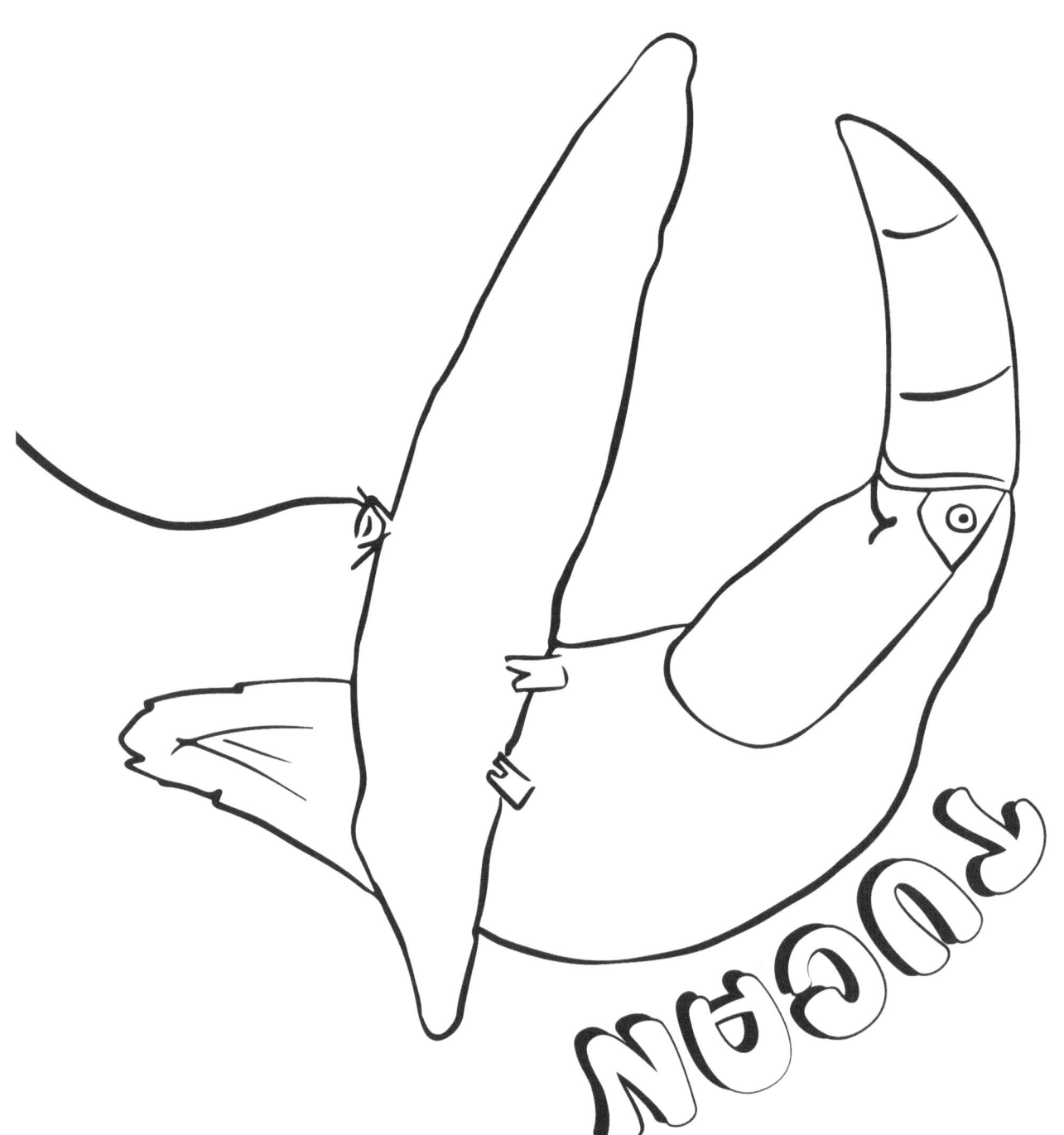

TUCAN

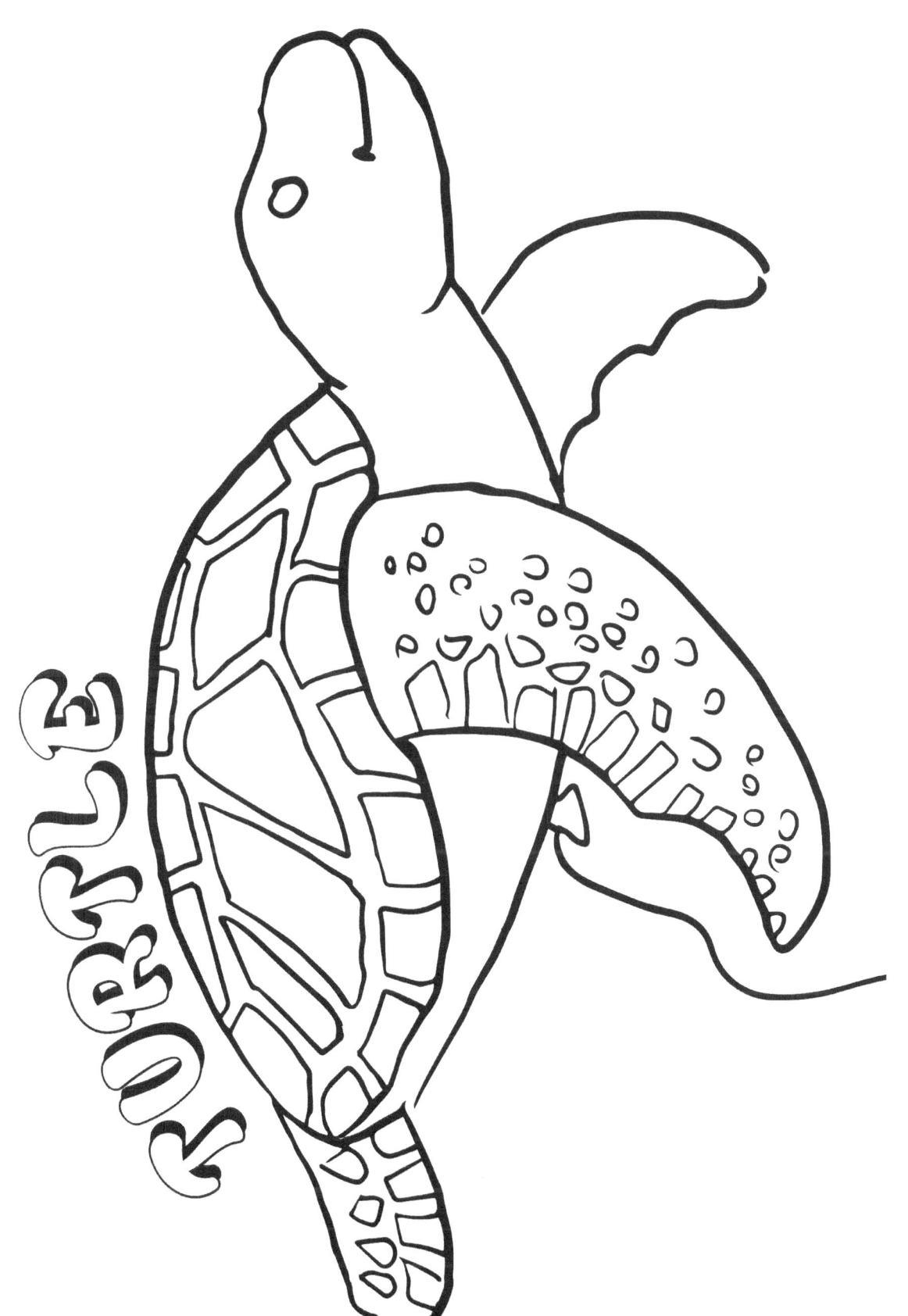

TURTLE

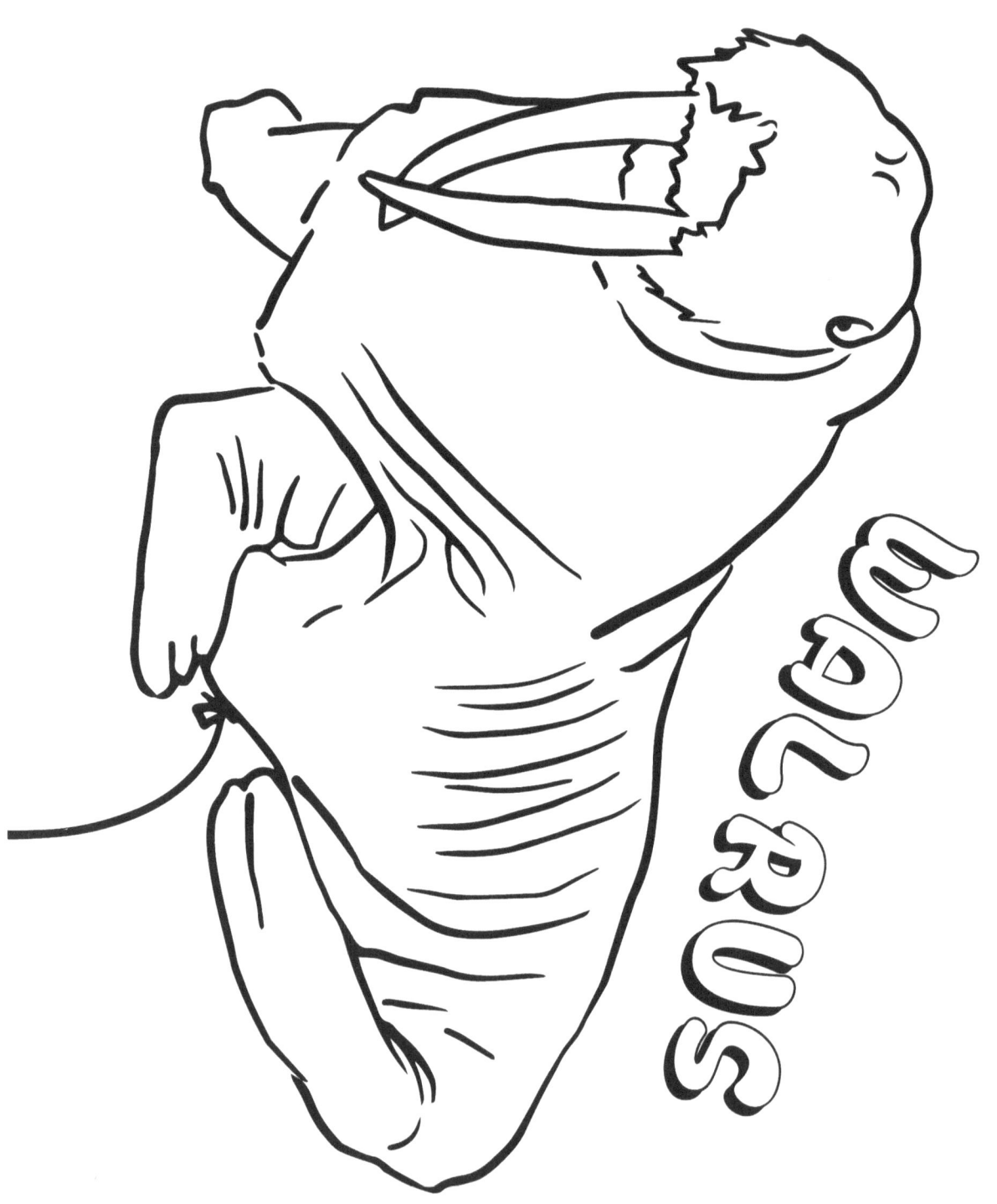

WALRUS

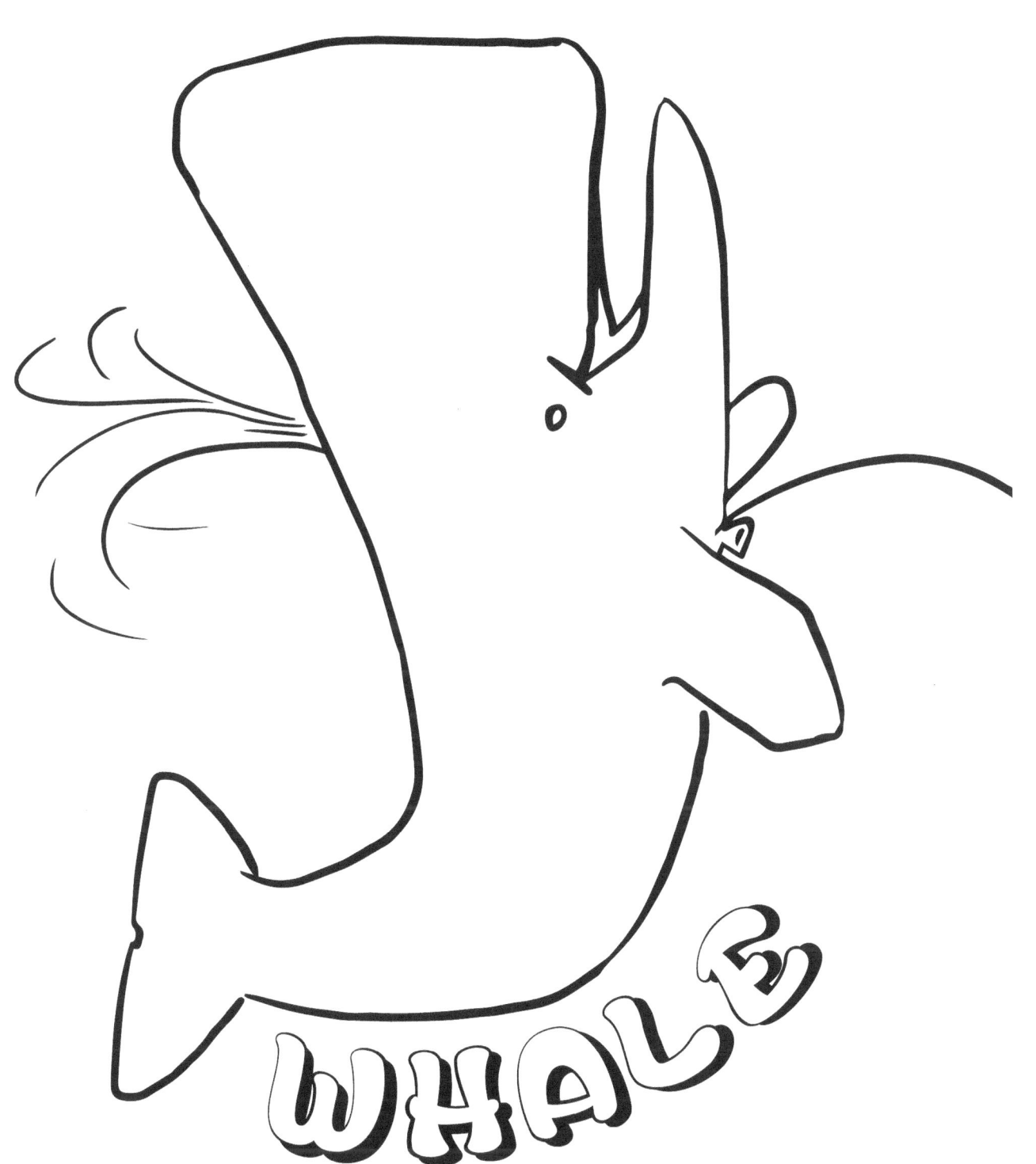

WHALE

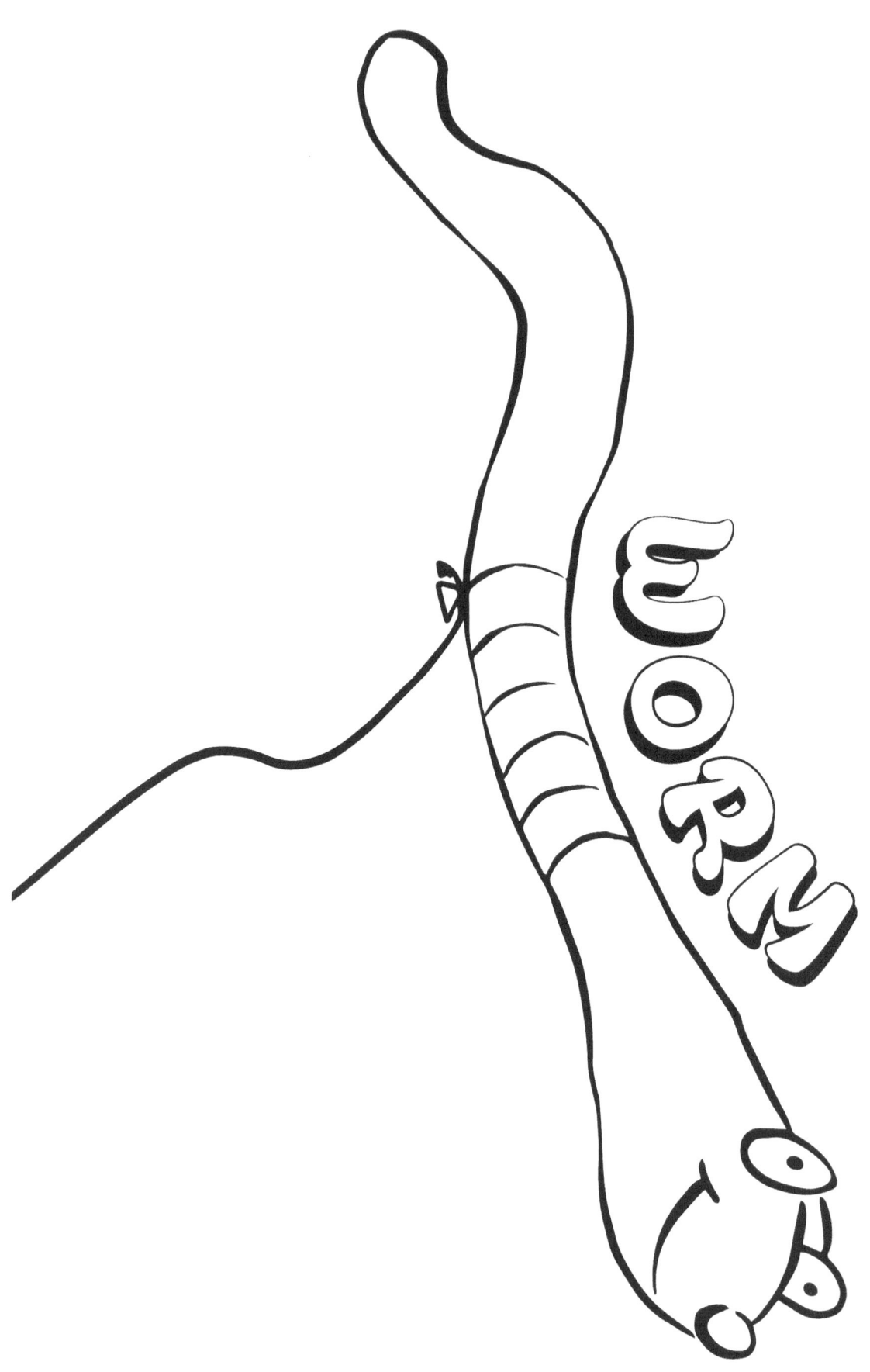

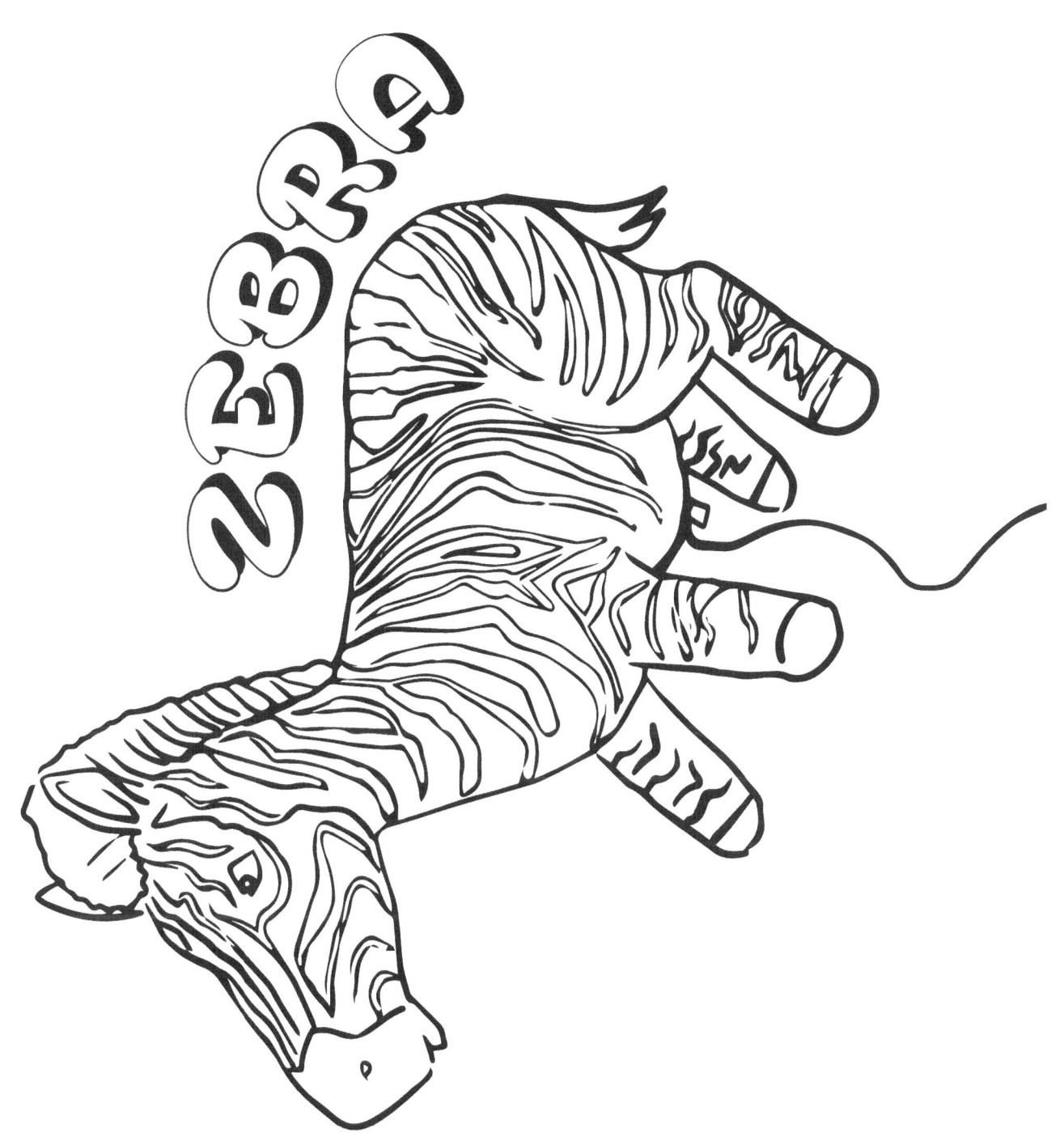

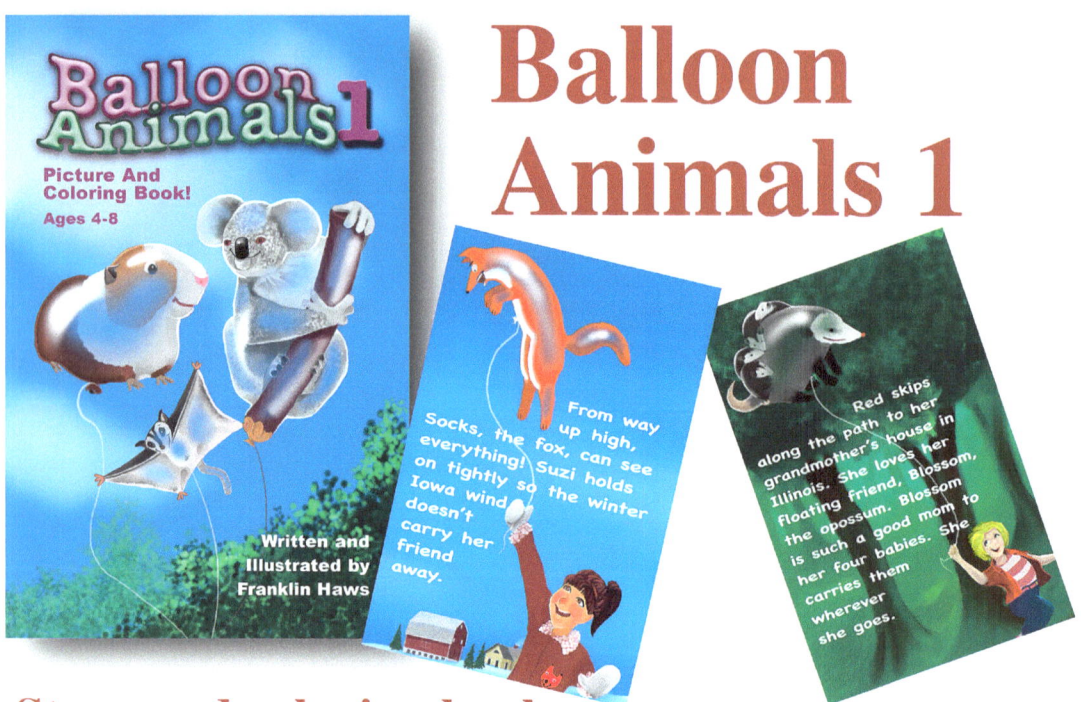

Balloon Animals 1

Story and coloring book.

Ages 4-8

If you love animals like chipmunks, rabbits or even the armadillo, you'll love Balloon Animals 1. Every page features a different animal but as balloons! And each having it's own cute story!

Available for the Kindle and iPad. (eBook versions do not include the coloring book pages) Print version can be found at createspace.com

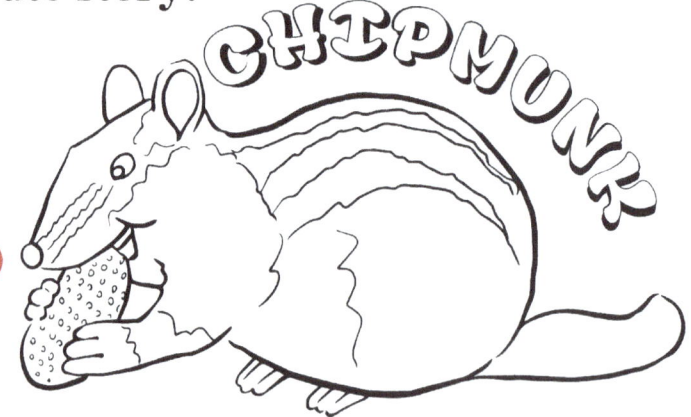

Written and Illustrated by Franklin Haws

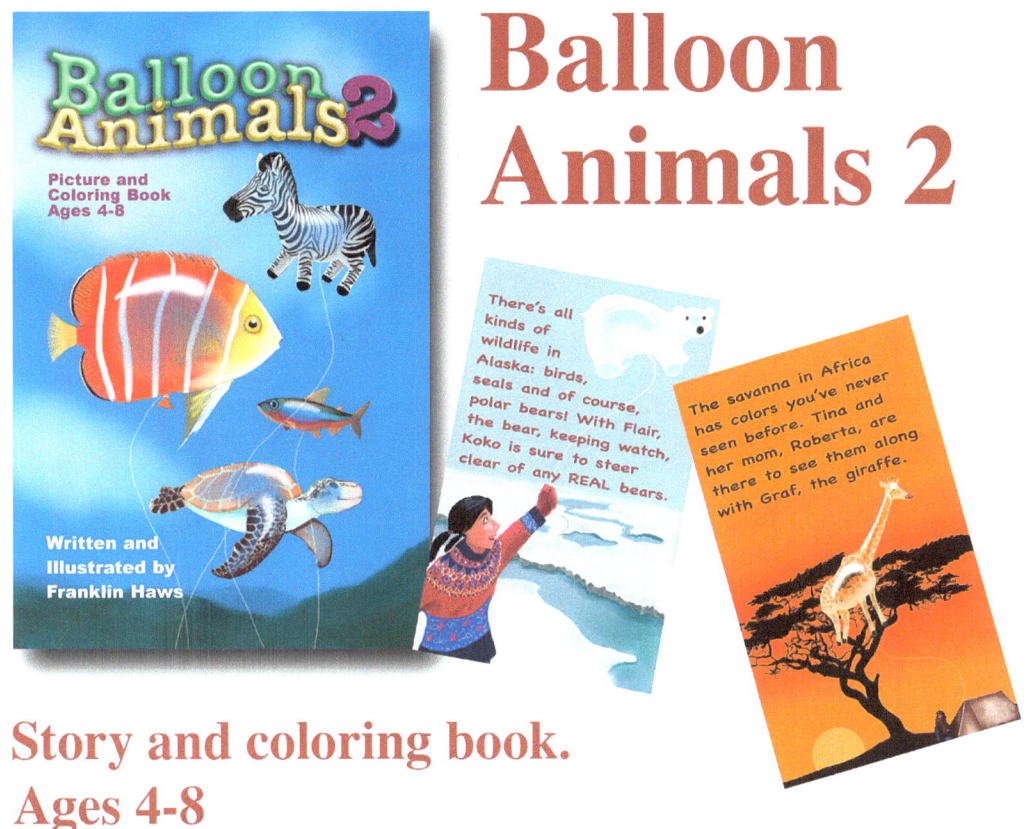

Balloon Animals 2

Story and coloring book.
Ages 4-8

If you love animals like turtles, toucan or even the mighty bison, you'll love **Balloon Animals 2**. Every page features a different animal but as balloons! And each having it's own cute story!

Available for the Kindle and iPad. (eBook versions do not include the coloring book pages) Print version can be found at createspace.com

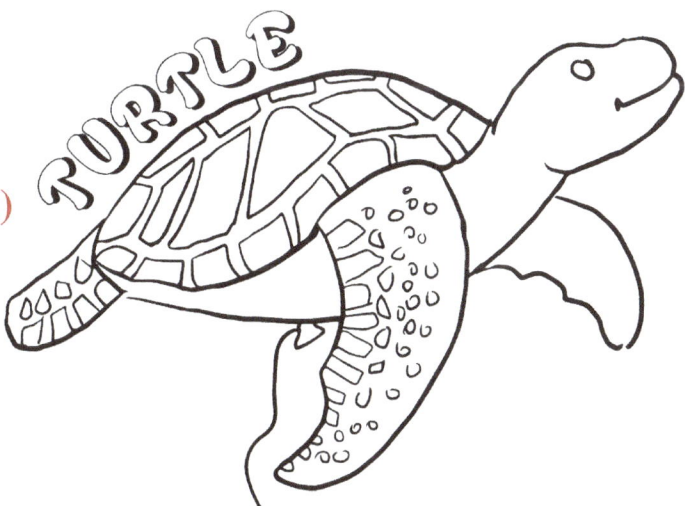

Written and Illustrated by Franklin Haws

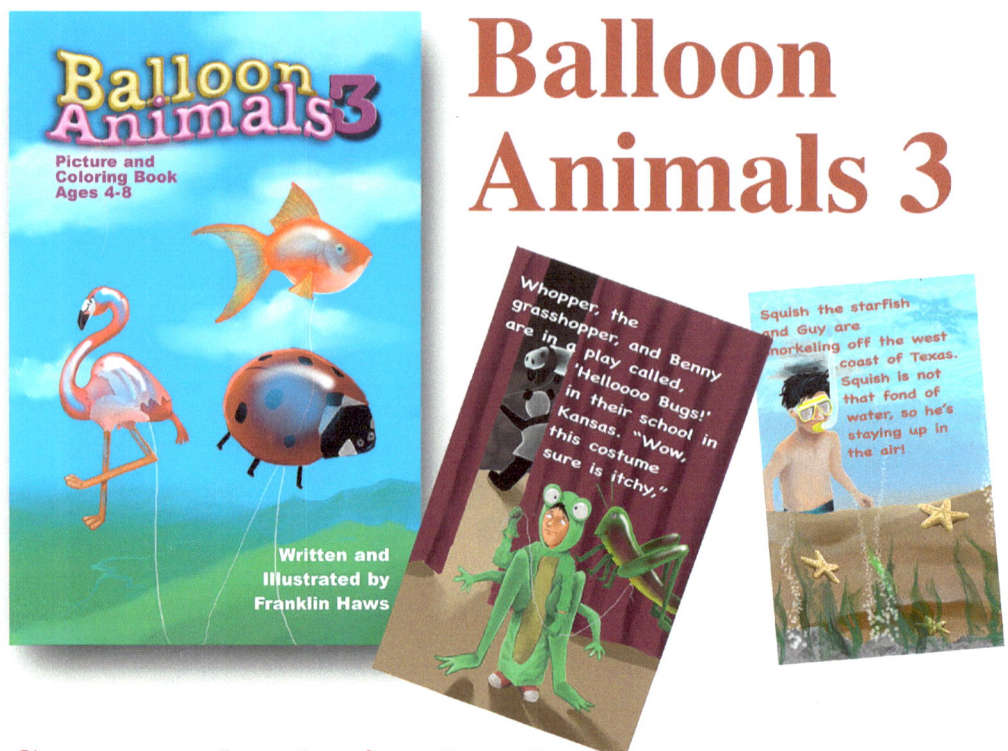

Balloon Animals 3

Story and coloring book.

Ages 4-8

If you love animals like ladybugs, owls or even starfish, you'll love Balloon Animals 3. Every page features a different animal but as balloons! And each having it's own cute story!

Available for the Kindle and iPad. (eBook versions do not include the coloring book pages) Print version can be found at createspace.com

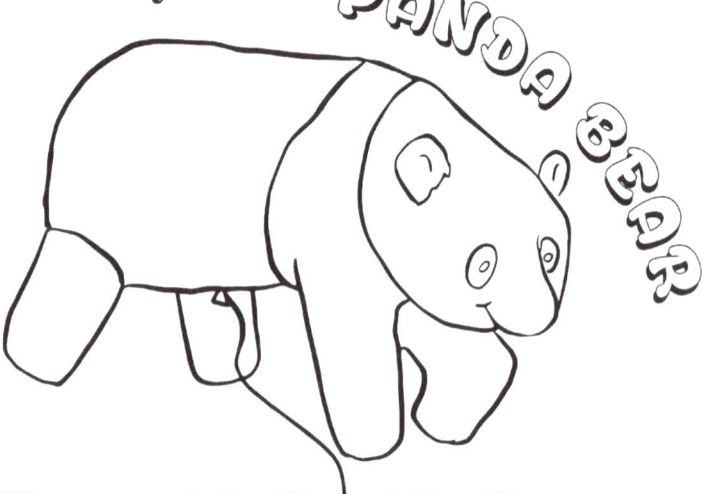

PANDA BEAR

Written and Illustrated by Franklin Haws

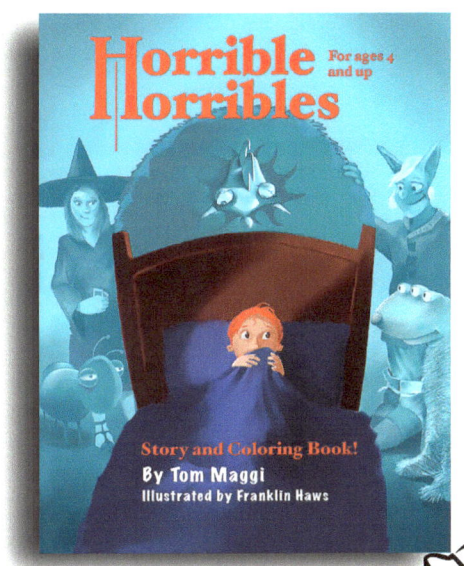

Written by Tom Maggi
and Illustrated by
Franklin Haws

Horrible Horribles

Story and coloring book.

This is a wonderful story of a young boy who has nightmares about scary monsters and space aliens but, he doesn't have to worry because daddy is near!

Available for the Kindle and iPad. (eBook versions do not include the coloring book pages) Print version can be found at createspace.com

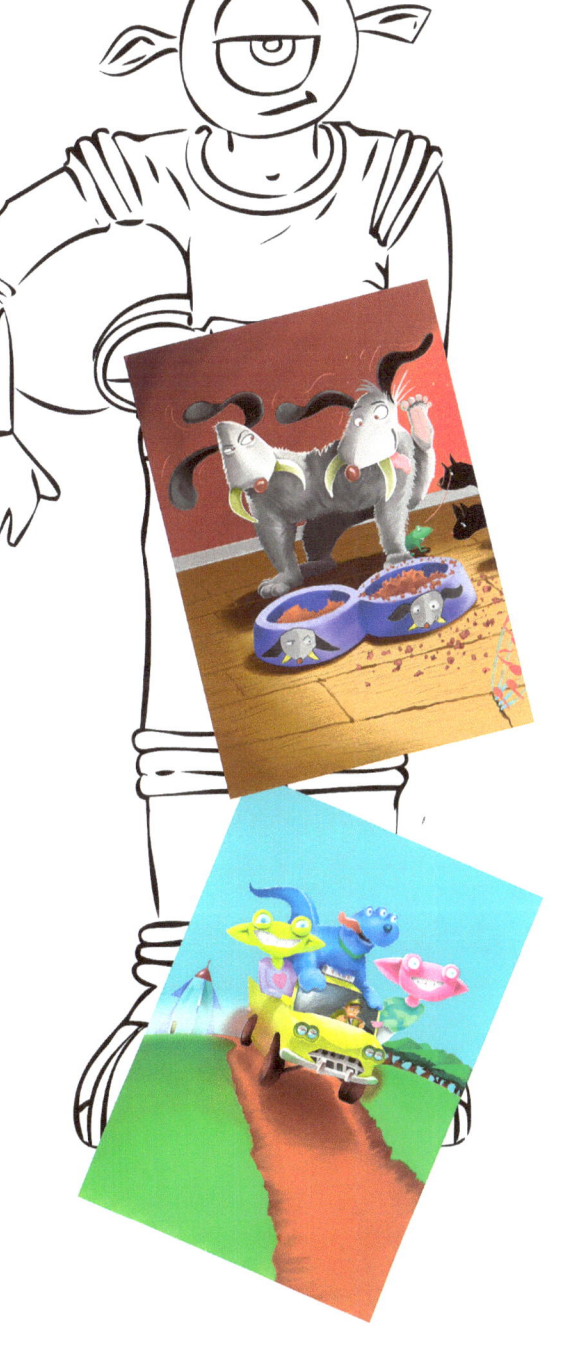

Franklin Haws
Digital Illustrator

Franklin Haws is a digital illustrator in the Minneapolis\St. Paul area.

Working exclusively with Corel Painter and Adobe Photoshop,
Franklin creates many types colorful illustrations ranging from automotive,
aviation, fantasy and children's books.

Humor and vivid colors are evident though out all
of Franklin's work.

Commissions welcome!

franklinhaws@hotmail.com

franklinhawsartwork.com/

zazzle.com/buyfranklinsart

zazzle.com/zenlifeandcurling

facebook.com/Franklins-Artwork

twitter.com/franklinhaws

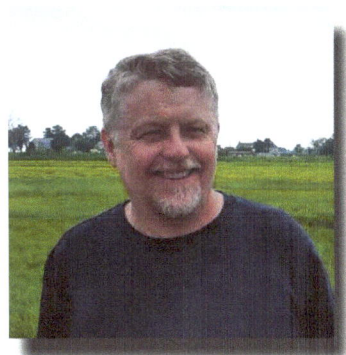

www.ingramcontent.com/pod-product-compliance
Lightning Source LLC
Chambersburg PA
CBHW050745180526
45159CB00003B/1360